# BEASTS OF BEING

## Partnerships Unburdened

## Maddy Butcher

**Cayuse Communications**

www.cayusecommunications.com

# Also by Maddy Butcher:

*A Rider's Reader: Exploring Sense, Science, & Sentiment*
*Horse Head: Brain Science & Other Insights*

**Find them at CayuseCommunications.com**

*The horse elevates us. Not just in altitude, but to a higher level of being.*
—Joel Nelson

*Properly speaking, there is no certainty; there are only people who are certain.*
—Charles Renouvier

# Contents

## PART I:
## The Science and Practice of Horsemanship

# PART II:
## Moving Toward Equanimity and Resilience

# Preface

I share personal opportunities for growth, life lessons, and horsemanship travails because I know readers have similar stuff going on. We're all works in progress, facing hurdles every season, probably every day. While the choices we make forge our unique characters and paths, there are undoubtedly universal connections in our specificities.

What you're holding is a collection of my work over several years. The loose parameter is "life with horses." As with the two previous books, *A Rider's Reader: Exploring Horse Sense, Science & Sentiment* and *Horse Head: Brain Science & Other Insights*, this book leads with the more academic and challenging research-supported topics. Steak before cake. The later chapters consist of essays more reflective and fun in nature. Some are drawn from mainstream journalistic work, like opinion pieces for the Washington Post. I hope all will be entertaining and engaging.

Often, us writers feel like we work in dark closets. Dark closets with little mail slots. After contemplation and multiple rewrites, we send our work out through the slots. How it's received, we can never be sure. What's rewarding is when someone opens the door, lets some light in, and says, "Hey, what you wrote was interesting. It reminded me of . . ."

In other words, when you reach out and connect with us hermit-y writers, it's wonderfully gratifying. It reminds us that, actually, we don't work in closets. Our work is not in vain. We're part of a community. Let me know what you think of *Beasts of Being*. I'll be happy to hear from you.

# Introduction

If you're like me, you are noticing more and more that in order to be good with horses, you need to be good with yourself. You need to work at your humanship along with your horsemanship. This book asks us to consider actions we might take to make this happen.

- Will we take a longer, more challenging path that involves unlearning bad habits while laying down better ones?
- Will we be honest with ourselves about fears and weaknesses in the saddle, in relationships, at work?
- Will we lift up our horses, our co-workers, our partners, and friends as we make our journeys?
- What does empathy feel like for us, and how does it play out in our lives and our lives with horses?
- Can we accept "best practices" supported by science and evidence, or do we conjure excuses to dismiss them out of hand?

I feel lucky and privileged to put these questions before you. We horse owners are lucky and privileged to have these First World "problems" and to have horses in our lives. And yet, being human is hard no matter your socioeconomic standing. Heck, some of us struggle with the "indulgence" of horse ownership. And that's just the tip of the iceberg when it comes to horse-owning angsts.

I have this image in my head of when I was 12. Bad haircut. Old cotton knit sweater worn thin by endless use. I'm holding my pony, Honey, by the reins. Tight under her chin. From the haircut to the horsemanship, I've progressed and improved over the decades. Perhaps the most important idea that I've come to embrace and that I ask you to embrace, is that it's okay to be wrong.

Like the history of science, our own private histories are littered with discarded theories, dust bunnies of wrongness. That's what the author Kathryn Schulz writes in her book *Being Wrong*. It's these scraps of experience and experimentation that shape a better you, a wiser you, a more capable you, a you with better hands and better haircuts.

When we're okay with being wrong, we become better listeners. We become more humble and open-minded. We get better at looking out at the world as well as looking in, to see our own biases and blind spots. When we acknowledge our unknowns and possible missteps, we not only learn more about horsemanship, we get to know ourselves better. My friend Kyla Strange, an accomplished horsewoman, talks about the "long heal" of working through life's challenges. For me, the idea of the long heal nicely replaces "long haul" as a more thoughtful and positive expression of how we move through our adult years.

Life is an ongoing conversation. As engaged riders, we can consider this idea: in order to have happy, responsive horses, we need to be well and aware. In other words, can we work at being happy and responsive humans? I think we can. I think horses, as beasts of being, nurture our evolution.

# PART I

The Science and Practice of Horsemanship

# CHAPTER ONE

# Of Horse Heads and Brain Science

A decade ago, I helped Steve Peters and Martin Black with the manuscript for *Evidence-Based Horsemanship*, a book that predates most of the horse brain science books available now. *A Rider's Reader* and *Horse Head* have chapters dedicated to brain science, starting with basic information about the autonomic nervous system and expanding to more specific explanation of things like memory, vision, and neurochemistry.

Knowing about brain science provides helpful insight when working with equines. It can often answer the "why" and "how" behind our more casual observations. It's hard to translate complicated science into something that readers can appreciate and apply. That's why I feel brain-science reporting has been important and worthwhile.

This chapter features select topics related to neuroscience, but does not review much of what's been previously published. If you'd like to learn more about horse brain science, let me know and I'll send you a copy of *Horse Head*.

## Feel: A Brainy Explanation

Years ago, I defined **feel** as an intense awareness of action and reaction. Feel is knowing how your thoughts, behaviors, and movements impact your horse. It's an ability to anticipate and influence your horse's actions and behaviors.

But what does that look like on a neurological level? We can turn to neurologists studying baseball players to help us decipher the brain science behind horse-human interactions. To understand it, let's first consider how one distinguishes different kinds of movement. The **motor system hierarchy** identifies increasing levels of brain involvement. At the bottom and most basic level, there are reflexes:

- a twitch
- a lower leg kick that happens when a doctor taps your knee just so

- an instant hand-on-hot-stove withdrawal
- catching yourself from stumbling and falling on your face

Reflexes involve the brain stem and spinal cord, primal parts of the brain that we share with all animals.

At the mid-level of the motor system hierarchy, there are simple or stereotypical movements. These are procedural movements we do all the time. Not a lot of higher-level brainpower is required to walk, open a door, or even ride, after you've done it for a while. The brain areas engaged here are the motor cortex and cerebellum. We are best at these mid-level movements if we are fit and if we practice.

The highest level of movement involves the neocortex and the basal ganglia, more evolved regions of the brain. Activations from these areas involve intentional movements of self-expression and complexity. When the neocortex and basal ganglia are involved, says Dr. Peggy Mason of the University of Chicago, the movement becomes a "meaningful action." Riders engage all levels of this hierarchy, and really good riders are especially quick at the higher-level brain processing.

How can research on baseball players inform our horsemanship? It's tempting to assume that players with the quickest reflexes are the best hitters. After all, most pitches are delivered in the time it takes for you to read a single word. But, in fact, most folks—professional ball players and the rest of us— have comparable reflex times. We're all quick. Our knees all jerk the same. Moreover, it turns out prowess at the plate doesn't have much to do with fast-twitch muscles or physique. As Zach Schonbrun wrote in *The Performance Cortex*, two of the very best hitters contrast starkly in their physical makeup: Aaron Judge of the New York Yankees is 6'7", 285 pounds, and José Altuve of the Houston Astros is 5'6", 165 pounds.

So, what makes a baseball MVP? What distinguishes a master horseman with incredible feel? It's the ability to process and act when they engage in those higher-level movements of the neocortex. It's called **rapid perceptual decision-making**. Great hitters are great not because they react quickly but because their higher-level brain processing is so fast that, in fact, they can afford to relax and wait.

Hall of Famer Rod Carew epitomizes great feel, says Steve Peters (who himself played Division I collegiate baseball): "If you watch videos of him at the plate, you can appreciate just how long Carew was able to wait to decide whether to swing or not. The swing is fluid. His hands are soft. His timing and feel are impeccable. He always seemed to get the fattest part of the bat on the ball."

A non-baseball perspective can inform us of the stillness and quiet involved in rapid perceptual decision-making, too. Consider a cat: Watch as it prepares to pounce. It is still, relaxed, and focused. It is taking in lots of somatic information (the movement of the mouse, the quality of the terrain, the light, the wind) and processing at lightning speed to inform a successful pounce. The successful cat has incredible feel.

The author, Schonbrun, explains that really good players produce or respond to "patterns of spatially and temporally distinct and interdependent neuron activations" in ways that are different than other people. Adds Peters: "Lesser batters get fooled. They will put the command to the brain stem and spinal cord to swing too early. Or, their processing from the neocortex will not be fast enough and they swing late or not at all." Great players with fast processing have the luxury of not executing the movement until the last moment. They can subconsciously say "wait, wait, wait" as they read the pitch. Players' reflexes are pretty much all the same. For those very good players, the processing speed is much faster.

How do we translate what we know about baseball players' reflexes to horse-rider interactions? A lot of our work around horses involves mid- and low-level movements. But feel involves taking in a vast spectrum of somatic information from visual input to proprioception to memory of past experiences. As this happens, the best riders may be uncannily quiet, still, and relaxed. It's not unlike the batter reading a pitch or even, say, the micro-multitasking of a good waitress. Are my horse's ears up? How light is my line?

What did he do the last time I gave him this cue? Is the wind bothering him?

The best horsemen recognize the fluidity of any situation with any given horse. They take it all in and react with a decisive movement to those patterns of spatially and temporally distinct and interdependent neuron activations cited by Schonbrun. As with Carew or the cat, the great rider's brain is "very busy processing everything, but it's not really thinking," says Peters. "The rider is reading and readjusting, but he or she doesn't have time to articulate what's happening. There are no words for it."

Great feel with horses takes practice, experience, and a special awareness. From a big-picture perspective, feel is the ability to be in the moment while also drawing on reams of prior experiences. If we think too much and try to bring in language and self-consciousness, we miss the moment for effective communication with our equine partner. Have fun out there. And be like another Hall of Famer, Yogi Berra, who said "you can't think and hit at the same time."

## The Autonomic Nervous System: You and Your Horse

Despite mammoth differences between horses and humans, we share some similarities in the very basic development and composition of our nervous systems. We both have **autonomic nervous systems** (ANS), the largely involuntary regulators of our organs, muscles, glands, and other structures. The **parasympathetic** and **sympathetic nervous systems** are the chief elements of the ANS.

Parasympathetic and sympathetic? Huh? Let's consider two scenarios:

### Outing A

You're out for a pleasant ride on a nice, sunny day. Suddenly, an angry bear appears in your path. The sympathetic nervous system is called into action (for both you and your horse). It uses energy:

• Your blood pressure increases.

- Your heart beats faster.
- Digestion slows down.
- Y'all beat feet!

The sympathetic nervous system is what we see in flight, fight, or freeze situations. When a horse has a sympathetic nervous system response, we see the whites of his eyes. His muscles tense. His nostrils flare. Some of that is linked to the tensing of the trigeminal nerve, which runs over the eye, down the face to the jaw. The trigeminal nerve also helps explain why you will see these signs (white eyes, tight jaw and lips) clustered.

## Outing B

You're out for a pleasant ride on a nice, sunny day. This time, however, you decide to relax, hobble your horse, and chill for a bit. There is no angry bear. You and your horse hang out in a meadow. He grazes while you read and ponder life. Now is the time for the parasympathetic nervous system to show its colors and save energy:

- Your blood pressure decreases.
- Your heart beats slower.
- Digestion moves.

The parasympathetic nervous system is exhibited in rest-and-digest situations. When a horse has a parasympathetic response, he licks his lips and, even if there is nothing in his mouth but saliva, he chews. He might blink and cock one of his legs. When looking at these two trail-riding episodes, we can also examine our differences. Here is where the horse's lack of frontal lobe development might actually put him in a better spot.

You, the rider, may come away from the Angry Bear experience with nightmares and baggage. Every time you return to that spot, hear a twig snap, see a picture of a bear, talk about bear encounters, or smell huckleberries, you freak. In studies of post-traumatic stress disorder patients, chemical etchings on the brain can have the effect of turning traumatic experiences into what researchers call **super memories**. Of course, it's also possible that you use your reasoning (frontal lobe stuff) to overcome whatever reactive responses you may have.

If the horse has enough good experiences associated with that meadow and with you aboard, he will likely override or look past this exciting episode (especially if no harm came to him). Such is life without a frontal lobe. As Yogi Berra might say, *If the world becomes good, the world becomes good.* Alternatively, the horse may indeed retain his fearful reaction for some time.

After Outing B, the rider may come away from the experience by attaching the meadow, the smells, the book, the horse all into one fond, romantic recollection. Rose-colored glasses are frontal lobe stuff. The horse, on the other hand, may recall that he got to eat at that meadow.

## Polyvagal Theory

Polyvagal theory is a relatively new explanation of the autonomic nervous system. Please note that what follows is theory and not yet supported by much evidence or peer-reviewed research.

For decades, we have considered the autonomic nervous system (ANS) as a feature of the brain stem, a primitive part of all mammalian brains. The ANS is comprised of the parasympathetic (PNS) and sympathetic nervous systems (SNS). We recognize these states when we and our horses are in rest-and-digest mode (PNS) or flight-or-fight mode (SNS). At this primitive and reactive level, our brains are quite similar.

Many model the autonomic nervous system as simple PNS and SNS light switches (albeit with dimmer adjustments). We can assess our horses as they toggle between two states, relaxed or stressed. But set aside that metaphor and make room for the more nuanced approach of **polyvagal theory**, proposed by Dr. Stephen Porges some 20 years ago. Porges is a Distinguished University Scientist at Indiana University and founding director of the Traumatic Stress Research Consortium. Porges championed a new interpretation of the ANS as it exists in the brain stem and expands throughout the body and brain via the **vagus nerve**, the tenth cranial nerve running from the head to other parts of the body and brain.

The vagus nerve is made up of three **complexes**, one sympathetic and two parasympathetic parts. If you're like me and benefit from imagery, replace those ANS light switches with three dials that move up or down perpetually as situations develop and environments change.

The **dorsal vagal complex** (DVC), part of the parasympathetic nervous system, is most primitive and activates a freeze-or-fold (collapse) response. Think of a brake pedal as a metaphor. When the DVC is highly activated, the brakes get slammed. The sympathetic nervous system, as with the earlier model of the ANS, involves mobilization. But unlike the earlier model, Porges sees any movement—play, sex, walking, as well as fight and flight—as a consequence of SNS activation. Think gas pedal as a metaphor for the SNS.

The **ventral vagal complex** is part of the PNS and, according to Porges, should be thought of as the softer brake. It is the dial that "provides the brakes that tempers the SNS just enough that play is fun and does not flip into fight or flight activation . . . It also allows social interactions to regulate physiology and promotes health, growth and restoration," says Porges.

One crucial element that polyvagal theory allows for is the "freeze" that we horse folks know well, but that the traditional ANS interpretation didn't directly address. Previously, the freeze response was considered a more conscious action. This idea has troubled researchers who knew, for instance, that rape victims were not making a conscious decision to freeze. Horses, similarly, were freezing when extremely frightened, sometimes giving the impression that they were "bombproof" when in fact they were ticking time bombs.

Polyvagal theory allows for what Dr. Bessel van der Kolk (author of the outstanding book *The Body Keeps the Score*) calls "a more sophisticated understanding of the biology of safety and danger, one based on the subtle interplay between the visceral experiences of our own bodies and the voices and faces of people around us."

For the last few years, Warwick Schiller, the Australian horseman based in California, has been focusing on relationship-building with his horses. As he likes to say: relationship first, then training. Discovering polyvagal theory has provided the science behind the evolving convictions of his work. "Basically, I figured it out, then found the science that backs it up," said Schiller. The new approach has changed everything. "It's relationship stuff. The difference it's made with horses has been huge."

Schiller now works first and foremost on fostering a safe environment. That comes from acknowledging the tiniest changes in horses' behavior as they interact: "When you are most present and noticing the littlest things," he said, "that's when they are most relaxed. When you have really good timing and feel, you are communicating well with them. You can ask for the smallest of things in a way that makes them feel safer." This approach has allowed Schiller to build up "social equity" and make bigger strides in training. "Think of safety as a foundation on which you ask for bigger things," said Dr. Steve Peters. "You can't get anywhere without it. That's what keeps the engagement. There is no social engagement between you and the horse if you push the gas pedal or the brake pedal too hard."

## Novelty and Neuroplasticity

Novelty is essential for the development and maintenance of a healthy brain. Just like the attraction of the primary rewards of food and sex, new information (in the form of smells, sounds, sights, experiences gathered) is something horses naturally seek.

The **substantia nigra/ventral tegmental area** (SN/VTA) in the brain stem is a midbrain element that researchers have dubbed the "novelty center." It responds to novel stimuli and is packed with the neurochemical dopamine. ("Substantia nigra" is Latin for "black substance." It is dark because of the density of dopamine-producing neurons.) Not surprisingly, the SN/VTA is closely linked to the hippocampus and amygdala. The hippocampus is known to store memories and the amygdala responds to emotional stimuli.

Researchers have found that novelty is closely linked to the natural inclination of reward-seeking. This makes sense evolutionarily: the more information an animal can gather about its surroundings, the more likely it is to survive and reproduce. Or, in horsespeak: I'm going to check out what's over the hill because the grass there might be awesome. And, heck, I might find more friends, too.

In the brain, activity in the SN/VTA is associated with increased levels of dopamine. That's good! Dopamine is a feel-good neurochemical connected with learning. Researchers have found that subjects perform best when new information is blended with the familiar, a bit like a dj's strategy of sandwiching new songs with the tried-and-true. We know that the plasticity of the hippocampus increases with the introduction of novel information and experiences. We know that novelty and novel experiences improve memory and open the door to better learning potential.

As horse owners and trainers, we should keep the following things in mind:

- Understand that changing a horse's environment and adding new elements to any session or outing is a good thing.

- Remember that neuroplasticity increases after novel stimuli are introduced, and use this optimal time to make new connections and advance a training challenge.

- Let your horse experience new environments or new obstacles in a way that maximizes a relaxed, alert level of attention. Got a new creek to cross? Take time to allow your horse to lower its head, consider the footing, and smell the creekside. Look for licking, chewing, head-lowering, and forward ears.

- Let your horse smell new equipment and touch it with its vibrissae (whiskers). Got a new saddle pad? Try gently placing the pad on its back and removing it, giving your horse time to relax (lick, chew, breathe out) and adjust to what might be a new experience.

- Let your horse move. Don't forget that horses feel better if they are not constrained. Moving—neurologically speaking and physiologically speaking—is an essential part of healthy, effective learning.

Colleague Amy Skinner, a Best Horse Practices Summit presenter and horse trainer in North Carolina, adds the following: "Horses that get used to new experiences and environments are much more teachable and less stressed in general. The horses I get in training who are used to everything being the same and have set routines become easily stressed with little changes, even to the point of colic. These horses are not happy, and it doesn't do them any favors to not expose them to new things."

**Neuroplasticity** is a healthy brain's ability to form and reform synaptic connections created through gazillions of moments. Every being, from a lab mouse to a horse to a human, is unique because of these moments and subsequent memories. They are experiences stored and recalled. Our capacity to maximize our neuroplasticity—to continue to learn, develop, and sharpen our skills—depends on how much effort we dedicate to the task and, as researchers are finding, what kind of effort we put to the task.

## Dopamine Details: Release and Reinforcement

For years, horse owners and riders have gravitated to the black-and-white straightforwardness of the **dopamine response**. Licking, chewing, and associated manifestations of this feel-good neurochemical are simple, visible indices of the horse's state of mind.

Consider horseman West Taylor. The Best Horse Practices Summit presenter works almost exclusively with wild horses and shared these insights:

Creating the dopamine release is all we focus on here at my place. It's not about getting a halter on a horse. It's about how many times the trainer can get the horse to lick and chew, thus leaving a result that the halter will end up on the horse.

I feel the horse is constantly asking the question of "Am I safe?" These are some "Am I safe?" questions: raising of the head, turning the head, moving the feet. The more times I can create a dopamine release answer of "YES" to this question of safety, the calmer and quieter the horse becomes. I'm working with wild horses, so this question of safety is at the highest level. I may create 30 dopamine releases before I get the halter on a wild one. For a more confident mustang, I may only be able to create a handful of releases before I get the halter on.

The same principle applies to leading, saddling, trailering, packing, etc. It's not about the saddle. It's about how many dopamine releases I can create before I actually saddle the horse. This approach of focusing on the dopamine release rather than saddling the horse causes us to release pressure a lot more often. In that way, we create a calmer, quieter horse. For example, I just spent two hours with a very cautious mustang, assisting him in finding safety while loading in the trailer. He was very explosive about even being presented with the idea of loading. He would pull back and explosively back up until he was completely away from the trailer.

In a period of two hours, I created 174 dopamine (measured by licking and chewing) releases before he loaded himself in the trailer. I feel that he created a "feel good" path from wherever I could first get him to lick and chew, all the way into the trailer. We paused with each step or hint of curiosity all along the way. This took patience on my part and curiosity from the mustang. I feel this dopamine process will make a lasting change in his mind.

But, as with everything, there are finer points and nuance to what, at first glance, is a simple concept. At least one trainer believes simple can quickly turn to oversimplified and be of great disservice to the horse. Too often, says Skinner, the rider may train her horse to routinely seek escape instead of relaxation. "I see a lot of people rewarding the wrong thing or training a horse to get in the habit of tolerating a request because at the end there will be relief." Consider a human scenario. Skinner gets uncomfortable at novel, crowded parties:

> I get a big dopamine release when I'm finally at home, having left the party. But it would be a better learning experience for me, really, if someone could nurture my ability to enjoy the party, to find a dopamine release within a big, crowded situation. Without that kind of training, more exposure to parties doesn't make me enjoy them more. It makes me resent them more. I may learn "acceptable behavior" so I can get out of there faster. I think a lot of horses do this with training.

Similarly, she likes to encourage horses to find relaxation (licking, chewing, breathing in a relaxed way) *during* the request or exercise, not after. She pays particular attention to a horse's breathing. She'd like it to be rhythmic, not shallow. The horse's barrel is soft and its legs move freely. The eyes and nostril are relaxed. "Like someone in a yoga class. Active, engaged, but relaxed," she said. Colleague Steve Peters weighs in:

> I agree with Amy that there is a big difference in learning in a relaxed state and finding relief versus escape from pressure. However, dissociation, involvement of the amygdala, and creating good learning experiences are all relevant here. What's needed is a more nuanced understanding of dopamine reinforcement.

We all know that we need to have their attention. Horses are not with us when bored, distracted, or stressed. But when stressed, they will often dissociate or check out. They may still hear our message to some extent, but they are not comfortable in their nervous system (e.g., jaw is still tight, eyes are not focused, etc.). Some messages we're sending are getting hijacked by the amygdala. The horse dissociates and we are no longer in sync, although the horse may appear calm. If you look closely, you'll see they are not comfortable in their bodies.

One of the critical underlying issues for our horsemanship is showing the horse how to get to a safe internal state. It is never about the tarp or the trailer or the trail, specifically. We need to show our horses how to search for and find this safe state no matter what is going on around them. The safe state is when messages are going through the motor sensory system and bypassing the amygdala.

Lead line and ground work can be especially helpful with connection through sensory messages that the horse can feel and understand. When the message is clear, the horse can begin to find safety in it. They become comfortable in their body. We also know that extra, "message-free" dwell time helps learning. Message-free time in our training allows the horse to make associations, consolidate information, and get the biggest dopamine reinforcement.

## Serotonin, Learning, and Dwell Time

When it comes to facilitating our horses' learning, new research is highlighting the importance of one brain chemical in the process: serotonin. Like dopamine, **serotonin** is a widely impactful neurochemical. We're most familiar with its connection to mood. Antidepressant medications, for instance, make more serotonin available in the brain. Oversimplifiers call it the "happy chemical."

Scientists in the United States, Portugal, and England, working with mice, found that its presence was vital for learning. As reported in the academic journal *Nature Communications*, mice were presented with reward-driven, decision-making tasks. They were given varying amounts of time to make decisions (generally of what to do and where to go to get a treat).

Through **optogenetic stimulation** (a technique that controls certain cells that have been modified to respond to light) of serotonin neurons, researchers found that those mice with stimulated serotonin neurons made "wiser" decisions and, broadly, learned more. But—and this is a big BUT!—those wiser, more circumspect learning patterns were only observed in mice that were given longer inter-trial intervals or breaks. Mice with shorter inter-trial intervals relied only on their last encounter with the task to make their decisions. Mice afforded longer intervals between trials made choices that were reflective of the greater scope of multiple trials.

## From Mouse Lab to Horse Pen

This research supports what I've learned about dwell time as being key to learning. Does your horse have time to make a decision or is it pressured? Does your horse get a break between asks and between sessions?

"Humans and horses alike need reflection in order to make associations," says Steve Peters. "If under pressure, the horse might only see and use one pathway. Essentially, it's just reacting. But under the influence of serotonin and the emotional homeostasis that comes with the presence of serotonin, the horse is better able to review the whole reward history and to choose from it and show the optimal behavior."

As horse owners and riders, it's up to us to let the light shine through. That's a geeky reference to the optogenetic stimulation used in the mouse lab. Of course, we're not keen on genetically modifying serotonin cells in horses' brains. But we can set up an environment in which our horses get time to lay down neural connections and cement associations. We can let them learn by letting them be for a serotonin moment.

## A Note about Dwell Time

When we use negative reinforcement to create a dopamine response (also known as **"pressure and release"**), we need to allow the horse to experience the **dopamine reward** (which may include licking and chewing, blinking, and head lowering) and to experience a **serotonin release** that facilitates its brain's ability to connect past experiences with new ones and to form associations.

That's learning happening. That's neuroplasticity. That's when good trainers get out their cell phones and reply to a text. That's when you might grab a long drink of iced tea. That's when you might say "good job" and put your horse away for the day. There is no golden measure of break time. It's not ten seconds and it's not one day. It depends and relies on your careful observation of your horse's behavior. It relies on feel.

There are microbreaks and macrobreaks. Microbreaks are moments between requests. Say, for instance, you are working on haltering or working on opening gates: Microbreaks are when the horse moves correctly and you release and pause. Macrobreaks are when you wrap up the training and stop for a day or more. Both are considered crucial to good horse work.

## The Hot-Cold Empathy Gap

This bit is about calm versus chaos, basic emotional states for both horses and humans. It was inspired by a *Hidden Brain* discussion with Shankar Vedantam and has much to do with the autonomic nervous system.

In the podcast, Vedantam explains that when we are in a calm, logical frame of mind, we cannot relate to our very same selves in an angry or fearful state. Nor do we connect with our cool, calculating selves when we're afraid. "Emotions completely transform us as people. So when we're in one emotional status, it's as if we're a different person than we are when we're in a different emotional state," he said. "We regularly lack empathy for ourselves."

This disconnect can be caused by situations as well as physiological states, like when we're hungry, hurt, or sexually aroused. The divergent states undoubtedly impact our actions and behavior. While the following example doesn't appear to relate to horse work, stick with me to see how it could.

In a research project, Dr. Julie Woodzicka, of Washington and Lee University, surveyed women about a prospective job interview. She told them that at some point, the male interviewer would ask inappropriate, sexually-oriented questions. What would they do? Nearly all the women said they would respond assertively, with anger and indignation, and would likely walk out of the interview. Dr. Woodzicka then invited other women to actually be interviewed for a job. During the interviews, conducted in a private, one-on-one setting, the male interviewer asked them inappropriate, sexually-oriented questions. Nearly none of these women balked. They answered all the questions, even the inappropriate ones, and stayed for the interview's duration. (They were later debriefed and told that they were part of a research project.)

If you understand the hot-cold empathy gap, you can see why this odd result was, in fact, predictable. According to another researcher, Dr. George Loewenstein, professor at Carnegie Mellon University and director of the Center for Behavioral Decision Research, we may consider two kinds of hot-cold empathy gaps as they relate to horse work.

**Prospective empathy gap:** You get nervous and reactionary when you attend a clinic. Looking forward, you say to yourself, it won't be this way. It's very likely that you'd be wrong. Researchers have found that people who've already experienced hot states are still bad at predicting their future behavior in a hot state.

**Retrospective empathy gap:** You don't understand how you got so frazzled at that last clinic. Looking back, you consider it an anomaly. "Our memories are faulty, especially when it comes to how intense feelings can overwhelm us," said Vedantam.

My friend Nina Fuller was interviewed by Vedantam. She lives in Maine, where she runs Lily Brook Farm, a 501 (c)(3) non-profit. She has a master's in Counseling Psychology with a concentration in Equine Assisted Mental Health and uses her horses in therapy work.

Fuller recalled a time when she and her husband were living in Washington, DC. She needed extra money and answered an advertisement for what seemed like on-the-job massage training. On her first (and last) day, she was put in a room, alone, with a male client who wanted more than a simple massage. How she acquiesced has troubled her for decades. Vedantam summarized Fuller's response: "She did not act assertively when she was frozen in place by embarrassment and shock." Fuller's actions were incongruent with what she would have imagined she'd do in that situation. Even after it happened, for years, they didn't make sense to her. She's just now learning how surprise, fear, and shock affect one's ability to act in the moment.

Just as we are consistently terrible at predicting how we'll behave in a different emotional state, we also struggle to relate to other humans when they're in a hot state and we're in a cold state. Or vice versa. The result is that we unfairly judge ourselves and others. In the case of us riders, we unfairly judge our horses, too.

Here's a scenario: My new horse, Barry, and I have been working on our partnership. The eight-year-old gelding came from a sorry situation. He's a nervous guy. After several months of quiet ground work and riding in my dry lot, we'd been enjoying getting out on the trail. During rides, I practice bending him and asking him for a one-rein stop at a walk and trot. We also trot and lope in big circles. I ask him to back, move his hindquarters, and sidepass. It's been great. If his ears, his breathing, and his licking and chewing are any indication, I'd say he'd agree. We feel connected, confident, and calm. But that all changed during one incident.

We were returning from a pleasant, two-hour ride. I had left a water bottle on a fence post and I stopped to pick it up. Barry made strange with this action and with the new, metal object just out of his field of vision. He started running. For 100 feet, I stayed calm but juggled the water bottle as I tried to slow him. I could feel him surge with energy as he moved into a panicked gallop. We raced toward a fence, where he'd have to go left or right. He went left and I came off.

I collected myself, collected Barry, and remounted. We rode for another 30 minutes, trying to return to a more relaxed and connected state. Afterwards, I chided myself: Where was that quick and ready one-rein stop? Why hadn't I immediately dropped the water bottle? Doing so would have given me two free hands and eliminated what concerned Barry. Why had Barry freaked out and ignored my direction? We might have been handling ourselves well in calm, controlled situations. But when the sh*t hit the fan, neither of us were able to quickly adjust. After the wreck, this weird, scary incident seemed to have no association with the partnership we'd built. Hello, hot-cold empathy gap.

Later in the program, Vedantam interviews Anastasia Fish, a second lieutenant in the U.S. Army. She explained her training to become an Army Ranger. The military calls one element of it "stress inoculation." It involves repeated training under duress. Soldiers learn to function well in high-stress situations.

When horses are in the sympathetic nervous system of fight, flight, or freeze, they will do whatever seems to be the right thing to survive in that moment. But we can teach them options. More importantly, we can teach them to self-regulate and find safety in hot states. But we must practice in calmer, more controlled settings first. Says Steve Peters, "Horses don't know how to emotionally self-regulate, especially in aroused settings, at which point they will be victims of their neurochemical state and default to flight, fight, or freeze. But if we show the horse how to mentally find safety during multiple training sessions of lower pressure, i.e., calmer settings, he will experience self-regulation. With more practice and increasingly higher pressure, he will learn to find safety as his new default."

When we can practice in increasingly stressful environments, we can build agility and confidence. Certainly, Barry and I have a new to-do list:

- We need to practice going fast without panic.
- We need to practice handling odd objects.
- We need to practice one-rein stops from faster speeds.
- We need to embrace unpredictable novelty.

These are all exercises we can do first in calm settings and then in increasingly livelier ones until we're more comfortable in hot states.

## Heart Rate Variability, I: Monitoring and Technology

As new devices like heart monitors become available for horse owners and riders, it's important to understand their potentials and limitations. Technology often outpaces our knowledge base, making the setting ripe for misinterpretation and misinformation. Take a moment to educate yourself and have fun in the process. Connecting with horses may be facilitated by a device, but it's always about taking time and being present.

People have been using heart rate (HR) monitors since they were clunky chest devices with thick, uncomfortable black straps. Wearing one made you feel like a hospital patient. As HR monitors have improved to slender smartwatches and Fitbits, it's become easier and easier to check your pulse whenever and wherever you want. Heart rate tends to be a simple and important indicator of fitness and wellness. Most athletes have a low resting heart rate. Their pulse may ramp up when they exercise, but soon afterwards it will slow. Through conditioning, athletes' hearts have become more efficient than non-athletes' at pumping blood.

More recent is the development of HR monitors for animals. For a price, you can monitor your horse's heart rate with your phone. Monitoring heart rate and respiration can be helpful for training and conditioning.

More recent still is the advent of **heart rate variability** (HRV) monitoring. Heart rate variability is what it sounds like: the amount a heartbeat varies over the course of many beats. You might think that if your HR is 60 beats a minute, then your heart is making one beat per second. In fact, it might be 0.97 seconds, followed by 1.01 seconds, followed by 0.99 seconds. HRV measures this variation. For my fellow junior scientists and dorks: HRV is the root mean square of the difference between heartbeats. Consider it a standard deviation calculation for a set of number values.

HRV, researchers have found, is regulated by the autonomic nervous system (ANS), that primitive brain feature we share with our equine partners. As neurologist Dr. Virgil DiBiase says, "The autonomic nervous system functions near the border of mind and body. Heart Rate Variability quantifies our ANS."

As a reliable indicator of activity in the autonomic nervous system, HRV can help measure our wellness and well-being. Broadly speaking, if your HRV rating is low, you may be more stressed or fatigued as your ANS may be in more of a flight-or-fight (sympathetic) mode. Low HRV rates are associated with lower survival rates from heart attacks. People with anxiety and post-traumatic stress disorders are also more likely to have low HRV readings. If your HRV is high, your ANS may be in more of a relaxed (parasympathetic) state. The high HRV might indicate resilience and readiness. Physical and mental fitness both contribute to preferable HRV readings.

For human patients, HRV scores are often calculated with an electrocardiogram (ECG) machine over a 24-hour period. Using this method, clinicians have found that low HRV can be associated with depression, anxiety, and poor overall health, while patients with higher HRV readings tend to have better cardiovascular fitness, respond more resiliently to stressors, and are better able to switch gears, showing more flexibility.

Dr. Andrew Flatt is an HRV researcher and professor at Georgia Southern University. His work focuses on monitoring athletes over the course of days and weeks. He says that "HRV will not be able to tell you precisely what the issue is, but it's a useful indicator that something is up, and intervention may be needed."

Katrin Silva is a regular guest columnist for me, a Best Horse Practices Summit presenter, and a competitive ultrarunner. She considers her resting HR for training feedback and relies less on HRV. "When my heart rate jumps up ten beats at resting, I know it's time to take it easy for a day or two. Maybe I need to recover from a hard run, or maybe I'm stressed, or maybe I'm fighting some respiratory bug. Or, all of the above. My watch uses HRV to calculate stress levels and training status . . . When my watch says I'm stressed, it's generally true."

You know things are complicated when mindfulness and athleticism each contribute significantly to how your heart rate is varying. Researchers try to account for the variables intrinsic to our lives and routines and how they feed into a deceivingly simple two-digit reading (average scores are between 40 and 70).

Horse-related HRV research is slim, but racetrack veterinarian Dr. Christine Ross has found that low HRV readings were a strong indicator of an upcoming injury or breakdown in racing thoroughbreds. Racehorse trainer Graham Motion was onto something when he said, nearly a decade ago, "a relaxed horse is a fast horse."

Can HRV monitors help us discern between training and overtraining? Can HRV distinguish between nervous excitement and anxious dread? Maybe. We learn more every day.

## Heart Rate Variability, II: Potentials and Limitations

Translating HRV data from animals is fraught with challenges. For starters, the waveform of electrocardiograms of hoofed mammals is not the same as ECGs of humans. Plus, most animals don't make good clinic patients. Just the simple act of moving requires scientists to devise a method for adjusting HRV readings to something meaningful and relevant while subjects are active.

In a study with sheep and cattle, researchers accounted for movement as "dynamic body acceleration" (DBA). They attached accelerometers (to record changes in DBA) and HRV monitors to their subjects. They discovered through calculated review that animals grazing on pasture were less stressed than those in confinements. They write: "We quantitatively and continuously confirmed that the stress levels of the free-moving animals within the grazing system were less than those in animals within the housing system, based on the results of the HRV analyses."

Those findings notwithstanding, slapping an HRV monitor on a horse and drawing immediate conclusions ("he's relaxed" or "she's anxious") is ill-advised. Consider, too, that when you are monitoring a device, you're necessarily taking yourself from full focus on the horse itself and the tiny changes in behavior (a weight shift, an eye blink, a breathe out) that might help you assess its well-being.

West Taylor, who runs science-based seminars, has presented at the Best Horse Practices Summit, and has an excellent understanding of how science can be applied to horse training, started using an HR and HRV monitor. While he's making observations and taking lots of notes, he's humble about his deductions and has visited many times with Dr. Virgil DiBiase, the aforementioned neurologist with a strong familiarity with HRV and the ANS. West writes the following:

> The biggest value I've found in monitoring HR and HRV is in waiting longer for the horse to fully mentally recover from whatever the stimulus was. I've felt like I waited a decent time, then I'd look at the HRV and see that the horse was still scoring in the sympathetic range (low HRV). Longer wait times result in deeper learning and calmness. My biggest take-away by far from using science-based horsemanship is: If we slow down faster, we get done sooner.

During a recent visit with Taylor, we placed HRV monitors on two of my horses. As supported by research, we found that higher HR correlated with lower HRV. More movement also meant higher HR and lower HRV readings, generally speaking.

HRV measurements are most valuable when the animal is resting and not valuable at all when the HR is over 120, said DiBiase. We worked accordingly: horses were standing or walking and their heart rates were not elevated when we monitored them. When HRV decreases, it's likely you'll see eyes more widely open and pupils dilated. When HRV increases, you'll see blinking and pupil constriction, DiBiase added.

Over the course of a few hours, we noted that when my rescued horse, Barry, was worried or surprised by a stimulus, his HRV decreased. It took minutes for his HRV to bounce back from a lower reading. We observed different HRV findings with my mustang, Bug: On a walk down the road, Bug noticed the sudden appearance of a man racing on a quad. Within a second, his HRV dropped from 80 to 40. In another few seconds, it bounced back to 80.

Does this mean the young gelding has an innate ability to self-regulate and deal with stressors? Is Barry less able to self-regulate and "get over" whatever he's stressed by? Maybe.

## Some Additional HRV Notes

As Dr. Andrew Flatt has found with his HRV work with human athletes, HRV monitoring may be most effective when used over weeks and months, not in the moment.

Racetrack veterinarian Dr. Christine Ross identified 13 at-risk horses by virtue of their low HRV scores over several weeks. Sure enough, 12 were injured or became ill in the subsequent months. The study has not been published, but Ross is working on a larger follow-up study to determine if HRV numbers correlate to a horse's susceptibility to injury or illness.

Dr. Ann Baldwin, of the University of Arizona, has found increased HRV values in humans when working with horses in an equine-facilitated therapy setting. She is studying whether physiological information can be exchanged between horse and human (like the correlation of HR and HRV readings of paired horses and humans).

Another study found that behavior and compliance to a task did not correlate to physiological stress. Researchers measured heart rate and heart rate variability, among other factors. Their findings may support the idea that horses can both comply and appear stoic while still being stressed.

Years ago, Dr. Temple Grandin labeled curiosity and novelty as key factors in working positively with livestock. HRV research confirms this: when animals investigate something new, their heart rate may increase, but so does their heart rate variability.

There's no doubt HRV monitors have the potential to be powerful tools for measuring physiological stress. If you do use one, try to keep your trials simple: How does HR and HRV change when your horse is being groomed? Can you correlate this with pinned ears, jaw tightness or, on the contrary, loose lips and blinking?

Hearts are not metronomes and brains are not blocks of simple dials and switches. HRV monitoring may become a handy tool in our horsemanship toolbox, but be wary of over-interpreting and oversimplifying its numbers. Your keen observation of a soft eye, steady breathing, and relaxed jaw (licking and chewing) may be more reliable. And infinitely more practical.

## Knowledge in Pain

*Redheads perceive pain differently than others.*

This fact, mentioned in "The Neuroscience of Pain," an article by Nicola Twilley, stopped me in my tracks. We know pain as a universal, yet universally confounding, phenomenon. Sure, some people seem "tougher" than others. But that gingers might have a genetic disposition to experience pain differently than others? Wow. The information helped me to appreciate just how nuanced pain can be.

More and more, I think of pain as a book. It may be a physical thing. But beyond that, it is a complicated brain experience. It is a series of multidimensional, neurologic episodes involving visceral feelings, past experiences, memories, genes, upbringing, and tangential distractions. What we know about human pain can give us insight into our horses' pain, its triggers, and the events and behaviors surrounding its pain. Most of the research supporting my writing is by Dr. Irene Tracey, head of the Nuffield Department of

Clinical Neurosciences at Oxford University.

Pain, of course, is experienced differently by different individuals. The same pain can also feel different to the same individual on different days, depending on a number of factors. Nonetheless, certain patterns are common in everyone, and pain "lights up" common brain regions. Consider the following elements of pain.

## *Anticipation*

In one of Tracey's experiments, a heating element was used to touch subjects with alternating burning or warm, pleasant heat. Different colored lights were associated with these effects. Soon enough, subjects learned to predict by the red, green, or blue lights what to expect: burning or warmth.

By using functional MRI equipment, researchers observed that more and more blood was flowing in specific brain regions (the **anterior insula** and **prefrontal cortices**) when the pain-indicating lights flashed. They learned that the "experience of pain could be created in part by anticipation, rather than by actual sensation." The study on anticipatory pain helped scientists break down the phenomenon of pain into more basic elements and determine where those elements are playing out in the brain.

We see an important parallel here with our understanding of pleasure, reward, and the dopamine response. As we become more attuned to a pleasurable scenario—like scoring well at an event or eating a cookie—our brains release dopamine in anticipation of the feel-good moment. Both pain and pleasure prediction make sense evolutionarily. It pays to avoid pain before it stings, just as it's valuable to pursue a time-tested reward. "Pleasure and pain. Two sides of the same coin," said Tracey. She likes to quote Jeremy Bentham, an English philosopher who died in 1832: "Nature has placed mankind under the governance of two sovereign masters, pain and pleasure."

## *Distraction and Subjectivity*

Researchers know that distraction diminishes the perception of pain. Concentrating on a tangential task (counting backwards as your doctor administers a shot, for instance) lowered activity in brain regions normally lit up on functional MRIs during pain experiences.

Undoubtedly, humans—and mammals, in general—experience pain differently depending on their environment, culture, upbringing, past experiences, as well as physiological and genetic predispositions (like having red hair). In one experiment, subjects were administered a fraction of discomfort while being shown an image of the Virgin Mary. Those subjects self-reporting as devout Catholics rated their pain lower than those identifying as atheists. Faith may engage some neural mechanism with analgesic benefits (i.e., somehow a subject's attitude can override a physical response). Depression, by contrast, tends to magnify self-reporting of pain, according to studies.

Over the course of years and multiple studies, Tracey and her team identified a cerebral signature of pain: distinctive and predictably recurring patterns acting in concert in specific brain regions during a painful event. In 2013, a colleague of Tracey's developed an algorithm that could recognize pain's brain activity patterns with almost 100 percent accuracy. Without asking a patient, the algorithm could help clinicians see whether a patient is experiencing pain and at what intensity.

## *Chronic Pain*

Something that starts out as conventional pain, say from a back injury, may not always look the same neurologically over time. Some pain can be good pain, the kind of pain that keeps you from doing something that would additionally harm you. Some pain, like chronic pain, can be bad.

When chronic pain sufferers and non-chronic pain sufferers were given the same pinprick, their brains lit up differently. "Once you've 'gone chronic,' as Tracey puts it, pain is the disease, rather than the symptom," wrote Twilley. Bad pain is not the result of any obvious external source. "Chronic pain, Tracey said . . . [has] a life of its own, with its own biology and its own mechanisms."

Researchers have found important mechanisms of chronic pain in the brain stem, located between the brain and the body. One mechanism muffles pain during events where you should feel pain, but don't (like winning a championship game after two grueling overtimes). The other boosts pain signals and seems to be more dominant in those patients suffering from chronic pain.

## Dog Brains and Breeds: Equine Insights

Mammalian brains—horse brains, dog brains, human brains—have many similarities. Since this is so, and since most horse owners love dogs, too, I thought you'd be interested in what folks at Harvard University have found.

Researchers there are discovering that dog brains have neuroanatomical differences depending on what they were bred to do. The differences have less to do with their outward appearance (like a big skull or a small body size) and more to do with regions of the brain that may be diminished or amplified, depending on which brain skills they most need. Dr. Erin Hecht is an assistant professor in the Department of Human Evolutionary Biology at Harvard University. For this study, published in the *Journal of Neuroscience*, she and her colleagues divided the brain into six components, or networks, involving such categories as drive and reward, olfaction, vision, and spatial navigation.

While the canine family tree is large and storied with hundreds of breeds, scent dogs from different branches of the tree have similar neuroanatomical traits. In other words, selective pressure through generations of domestic breeding have resulted in the same amplified or diminished components. Over the last 200 years or so, we humans have bred dogs to be good at various skills to help us get along and accomplish tasks. We've bred them to be good at herding, companionship, sight hunting, scent hunting, and guarding, for instance.

The cute Yorkie that's constantly in a woman's arms? The part of the Yorkshire terrier's brain that has most to do with social action and interaction has **covaried** (changed together) with the development of that breed, Hecht and others have shown. Meanwhile, the region of the Border collie and English pointer brains associated with drive, reward, and vision has covaried with the advancement of these breeds. Does this help explain why your Border collie and pointer thrive in open, working (i.e., reward-filled) environments and why your Yorkie is okay just hanging out? Yes! "The anatomy of these networks correlates significantly with different behavioral specializations such as sight hunting, scent hunting, guarding, and companionship," wrote Hecht.

What happens over the long course of time when breed-specific traits aren't used, essentially becoming neurologically dormant? What happens to the herding dog who lives in the city and whose puppies and then those next puppies never lay eyes on cows or sheep? Hecht is studying that, too. "We know that training is doing something," says Hecht. "We're trying to figure out how far an innate genetic inheritance gets you. And then, what's the additional bump that you'd get from experience and learning?" Can you take a city slicker Border collie, put it on a herd of cattle, and watch the magic unfold? That's not likely. But chances are, it would adapt a lot better than, say, a poodle or golden retriever.

Since Dr. Hecht's research on dog brains and how breed can manifest in canine neuroanatomy got my attention, I visited with her via email. We talked about how her insights might apply to our horse world.

MADDY BUTCHER: Ranch horses are valued for their ability to move cattle quietly and react quickly to a changing environment, especially in response to cattle movement. There are horses who outmaneuver cows without a rider on board. Or, a horse who keeps a mother cow away without instruction as the rancher tags her calf. Would you suspect that this trait is largely taught or largely in place neurologically speaking?

ERIN HECHT: This is a very interesting question which could be answered with research. Looking across the animal kingdom, some skilled behaviors are largely innate, with little learning required. One example of this would be web-making in spiders.

In other cases, skilled behaviors rely heavily on experience and learning during an individual's lifetime. An example here would be language use by humans. But even in those cases, there are often innate biases that help facilitate learning – a predisposition to attend to certain aspects in the environment, or to be drawn to or to try to avoid particular situations.

In the case of human language learning, babies show early predispositions to attend to adults' vocalizations and to babble, both of which probably help canalize their language learning along a productive path.

I would speculatively hypothesize that something similar might happen with ranch horses – some biases and predispositions are innate, and these shape individual animals' learning experiences in a way that helps produce functional skill.

MB: Gaited horses naturally have different stride rhythms than non-gaited horses. For instance, a Tennessee walker has a "running walk" that is completely different than, say, a trot or canter in a quarter horse. Can this be explained neurologically? Is gaitedness simply a widespread genetic mutation?

Also, temperament is a big deal in the horse world. Even the span of breeds is from "cold-blooded" to "warm-blooded." Cold-blooded are draft horses who are typically big, slow, and calm, while hot breeds like Arabians are more slight-framed and flighty. Would you suspect that their brains look very different, based on their temperaments?

EH: All behavior, including gait and other forms of locomotion, comes from the nervous system. So, if you have two different types of animals with different behavior, then there must be something different about their nervous system.

In the case of our 2019 dog study, differences in brain anatomy were pronounced enough to be measured with MRI. But brain differences at a much finer anatomical level can also produce differences in behavior. For example, differences in the distribution of receptor types can alter the way that brain regions respond to different types of neurotransmitters. This can produce noticeable differences in behavior – like whether a species forms pair bonds or not, for example – but it would only be detectable by examining brain tissue at a microscopic level.

## It's Not All about Brain Science

*The world will never starve for want of wonders; but only for want of wonder.* —Gilbert Keith Chesterton, 1874–1936

Like you, I'm curious. New information around horses fascinates me. Sure, I have the natural skepticism of a journalist. But when insights clarify and help improve our connection with horses, I'm all for it. Ten years ago, I caught the neuroscience bug. What I learned while helping Dr. Steve Peters and Martin Black with *Evidence-Based Horsemanship* undoubtedly improved my horse work. My subsequent research for *Horse Head: Brain Science & Other Insights* did so, too.

Now, though, I'm seeing brain science in a new light. No longer do I see it as the most essential know-how for a horse owner's educational toolbox. Like a doctor's assessment of a patient's physical appearance, it's just one part of a much bigger picture.

What we know about horse brain science—that licking and chewing is a parasympathetic response, that dwell times enable faster learning, that consistent dopamine-related experiences can build optimal learning patterns— can help us see what's going on and can hasten our progress. No doubt. But in focusing too narrowly on neuroscience, we run the risk of missing other equally vital components of the horse's development. We can neglect considering its overall well-being, its body, its life. Sure, it's helpful to zoom in to see the horse at a molecular, neurochemical level. But it's equally valuable to pan out for the big picture.

Before the Best Horse Practices Summit in Maine, I was chatting with keynote speaker Steve Budiansky about the other presentations. I mentioned brain science. There was an audible pause. Do you have reservations about that, I asked? He said something about it being a bit reductionist and we moved on. After the Summit, I got back in touch with Budiansky and asked him to elaborate. (**Reductionism**, in case you were wondering, is the practice of describing complex phenomena in simplified terms.) Steve was kind enough to expand on his thoughts:

> I am in general a great friend of reductionism, but I think it's a well-established rule that trying to understand any system as complex as animal behavior always demands multiple levels of explanation. It's certainly true that all animal behavior is fundamentally neuroanatomy—but that's also trivial and it doesn't really help us in itself to build up a useful picture of what's going on.

The way neuroanatomy is expressed in behavior is constantly limited and channeled and shaped by learning, environment, social interactions, all of which have their useful concepts and terminology that help us make sense of what's going on and why, and understanding how horses learn and react to different situations.

You could similarly say that all you need to do to win at chess is to know the rules of how the pieces move. True enough, but it doesn't get you too far.

I'm reminded of a typical summer scene in which I move through a gate to halter one of my horses. Yes, I'm watching for brain-science markers that can tell me how my horses are feeling. But I am also watching how they situate themselves among their herd mates, how the flies are aggravating them, when they last ate, and so on.

As students of the horse, we must cultivate our holistic awareness. We need to recognize that neuroscience, physiology, herd dynamics, fitness, and digestive health all matter and all merit study. There are myriad elements in any horse-human equation. Some we can quantify, some float under our radar. Are we aware of how much our presence impacts the horse? What about our neurology? What about how we treated the horse in the past? What about our fitness and mental health on any given day?

A friend of mine, who went to college and received his PhD in human sciences, is getting fed up with Western medicine. (For the most part, it's the system in which medical doctors treat symptoms and diseases using drugs, radiation, surgery, etc.) Eastern medicine, on the other hand, treats the whole person, encouraging a healthy body to prevent illness and speed recovery. My friend quoted Victor Hugo, who said, "Science says the first word on everything, and the last word on nothing."

He and Hugo have a point. Science helps us see things from a focused, hyper-informed perspective. It often gives us a brilliant new lens through which to interpret behaviors, interactions, and experiences. But if we fail to appreciate the whole person, the whole horse, the whole environment, the whole moment, we can get into trouble.

As Budiansky says, "I worry especially about the potential for mischief (and voodoo) in encouraging people to think you can leap from a few measures of the physiology of the nervous system to horsemanship. Neuroanatomy is very helpful in showing us what's wrong with certain ideas about training or horse behavior. But there's no magic shortcuts, and that's what I think we need to be on guard against."

# CHAPTER TWO

# On Riding and Horse Ownership

Studies show that horse riding is one of the riskiest activities we humans do. Riders assess and mitigate risk all the time; being safe is an integral part of riding.

## Safety Matters

With help from my friends Julie Kenney, Katrin Silva, and Amy Skinner, I offer these safety checklists as a way to assess risk level. Lots of us don't wear helmets. Lots of us aren't as fit as we used to be. Be honest about your risk assessments and consider altering your routine to be safer.

### *Key Questions on Safety*

- Are you riding with someone, or do you have someone around when you are riding? Alternatively, do you have a cell phone and reliable service where you're riding?
- Are you a fit and balanced rider? Can you mount from the ground? Can you mount from both sides? Can you trot, canter, and gallop with your horse?
- Do you know your horse? Do you have experience with this horse? Do you know his strengths, fears, tendencies, and weaknesses?
- Do you know yourself, your fears, your weaknesses, your ability to connect with this horse and deal with any potential crises or unexpected developments?
- Do you know your environment? What are the likely variables (weather, terrain, traffic, aggressive dogs, etc.) that might complicate or endanger your safe ride?
- Are you wearing a helmet as well as a protective vest?
- Can you stay balanced if your horse leaps or stumbles or slips (without yanking on the reins or inadvertently spurring him)?

- Have you checked your equipment? Good, well-fitting gear helps optimize any ride. This includes, but is not limited to, a saddle, bridle, boots with heels, leggings (especially if traveling in rough country), and a hat or helmet.
- Can you ride comfortably at all gaits? Can you handle an unexpected gallop?

There are pros and cons to riding with others, writes Katrin Silva. "Are you riding with folks you know and trust? Don't ride with people who have no control over their horses, who are not mindful of the abilities of the weakest rider or the greenest horse in the group, or who gallop past you without warning."

## Some Finer Points on Safety

- Can you read and respond to what your horse is expressing?
- Are you present? If you're distracted you can't relate to your horse. Most accidents aren't really freak accidents but a series of missed warnings.
- Have you prepared the horse for whatever experience you plan to give it, as well as unexpected ones?
- Do you know the horse you're riding TODAY? A horse on a hot day, in a familiar environment, who has been worked consistently for the last five days will not be the same horse after a week off, on a cool, windy morning in an unfamiliar environment.
- Do you know yourself as you are TODAY? Being able to sit a spook or buck at age 27 does not mean you can still do this 30 years later. When you're sick, overly tired, or emotionally out of sorts, or preoccupied, you won't ride your best.

Silva says it best: "There is no shame in getting off a horse at any point, or in not getting on in the first place. Many wrecks happen because of the human ego. Ride the horse you have today. Be mindful of the mind and body you have today. Ride in wisely chosen company or none at all. And don't let your ego get in the way."

## Diagnosis Offers a Eureka Moment

In horse work, the cause of an issue may live under layers of misunderstanding and ignorance. The effect, however, might be obvious: my horse balks at the canter, my horse drifts left, my horse acts aggressively with other horses. Getting to the root source of these problems can be a long, convoluted challenge of awareness, education, and trial and error. The journey is rewarding, especially if the "fix" improves the horse-rider partnership.

This is a short story about a long path to address the root cause of a riding problem. My riding problem: my horses drift left.

If you were to look at my back while I bent over to touch my toes, you'd see what appears to be a lot more muscle along the right side of my spine. You might think, as I did for years, "Well, you're strong-but-lopsided. You must do everything with your right arm and your right side." I tried to compensate. I'd shovel manure, toss hay, and carry saddles with my left arm. Still, my back seemed muscle-bound to the right of my spine.

After yet another hamstring injury put an end to my running routine, I sought out the best physical therapist I could find. Maybe the asymmetry had something to do with other issues, like this hamstring pull. A Big Picture assessment was needed.

At the initial visit, I must have sounded vague and clueless: Yes, the hamstring hurts, but sometimes the pain drifts up to my gluteus maximus or forward to my quad; the leg didn't hurt too much, but the pain prevented me from running. Other activities, including riding, weren't a problem at all. Was I so hurt that it required seeing a physical therapist? Coming from the tough-it-out-and-don't-complain camp (so common in my native state of Maine and in the horse world), I had guilt for even being in a doctor's office. Dr. Ellen Tomsic looked beyond the hamstring concern and identified the root cause: scoliosis.

Scoliosis, or curvature of the spine, is pretty common, affecting about 2 percent of the population. It's more common in women than men and can run in families. You can't cause scoliosis from carrying heavy stuff, being a competitive athlete, or having poor posture.

My back curves left. The right side isn't more muscular at all. When the spine curves left, it also rotates. So the right vertebrae bulge out while the left side rotates in. For years, Tomsic told me, my various muscles have been compensating for the irregularity. The psoas (deep core muscles that attach lumbar vertebrae to the femur) and hamstring, for example, have been constantly working to pull and straighten the spine. After so much strain and overwork to compensate for the curved spine, and especially when trying to handle added activities like running, these muscles had, in Tomsic's words, "given up the ghost."

Eureka! I felt like I'd won the lottery. Sure, having scoliosis is not exactly good news. But it gave me an answer as to why, over the course of my adult life, I've had back and neck pain, why I've been susceptible to peripheral injuries like hamstring pulls, why my shoulders aren't level. And, most importantly, it answered why my horses drift left.

Why? Because the spine curvature and rotation results in my having more weight in my right seat bone. That translates to more right-side pressure for my horses. In turn, they move off that slight pressure and to the left.

Physical therapy is now designed to do two things: mobilize my spine (which has become rigid and tight over time) and strengthen my core to support the spine. I'm learning how to really, truly strengthen my core, paying attention to the deep muscles of the pelvic floor that most of us athletes neglect even while doing conventional abdominal workouts. I'm learning that tiny, precise exercises to address weaknesses and rigidity can be waaaay harder than the standard routines I've known so well. "If bigger, better, stronger, faster were the answer, you wouldn't be here," said Tomsic. Lots of athletes run, ride, hike through pain. We think things will work themselves out. Until we can't anymore.

Drilling down to address the root cause of any issue is not like taking a course of antibiotics. The investment and attention is deeper and more protracted. It's more like making a life choice to be a healthier eater. These exercises will need to be incorporated into my daily life *forever*. It's a task I'm happy to do, especially if it means better athleticism and connection with my horse.

## Are You in Horsemanship Debt?

In an article on the complicated nature of California's wildfire problem, reporter Quinn Norton talks about technical debt. She writes, "Technical debt is the shortcuts and trade-offs engineers use to get something done either cheaper or in less time, which inevitably creates the need to fix systems later, often at great cost or difficulty."

Sound familiar? Horsemanship debt happens, too. What kind of debt are you incurring? When and how will this debt come due? Examples of debt coming due in the greater world include things like poor forest management contributing to the increase in massive wildfires, poor home building leading to expensive heating and repeated maintenance, and neglect of your physical and mental well-being leading to health problems.

Debt is what happens when you overlook small steps on the way to a bigger goal. Debt happens when you focus too narrowly on the task at hand. Think "blinders on." Debt happens when you rush through steps in the name of accomplishing what you told yourself you wanted to accomplish on that day, week, or given season.

I've been guilty of technical debt with at least two equines: I wanted to get to riding Jolene so badly that I rushed the process. At the time, I reasoned with myself. "I got this," I said with nervous energy. The first two wrecks should have been warning enough. It took a more serious one for me to pay attention to what my mule had been telling me for months: *we're not ready to go there.*

More recently, I've worked with Barry, a rescued Tennessee walker who endured harsh handling and neglect for years before I acquired him. After lots of ground work and paddock work, I started trail riding with him. Then a bolting incident made me realize my methods were wrong. I would need a different and more patient approach.

In both cases, at first I tried to rationalize my motives and missteps. I tried to justify what I'd done and tell myself that the incidents were just flukes and that my horsemanship was sound. But, as Norton writes, "skipping past anger and bargaining and even depression, all the way to acceptance of this new reality, and getting to work, is the best we can do."

The faster I can accept my missteps, the faster I can address the real situation. It is a logistical, skill-based process, but it is also an emotional one that requires shedding one's ego and preconceived notions. The more quickly I'm able to address the real picture, the better I will be at getting back to work. In this case—as in so many with our horses—it will involve going more slowly and thoroughly.

## Tragedy, Then Fun

First, the tragic.

I've been riding my new, nervous horse, Barry. We're making wonderful progress. But as summer heats up, I've noticed my saddle pad leaving sweaty, uneven marks on his back. The marks are indicative of poor saddle fit. I've tried to deny it and to comfort myself with these notions: It's an otherwise well-made saddle that should be comfortable for him, even if it doesn't fit him perfectly; he's big and I'm not so heavy as to cause him discomfort; he doesn't do anything obvious to indicate that he's uncomfortable.

Two pivotal developments tilted me toward a reckoning.

My friend and chiropractor Kathy Klix visited Barry, and she noted how sore his withers were. Given that he's completely sound, with good musculature and healthy feet, saddle fit got the pointy finger. So I contacted Elaine Welland at Western Sky Saddlery in Carstairs, Alberta. Over the course of several days, she reviewed images of Barry with and without my saddle. I even sent her images after a sweaty ride. "I know exactly what's happening," she said by phone.

Basically, I've been using saddles that were built for horses with straighter (flatter) backs. Barry has high withers and a back that angles a bit up toward his butt. He needs a saddle with more rock in it and perhaps a pad with greater contour. So I've started the process of acquiring a better saddle for this lovely gelding.

Next, the fun.

While bemoaning my wrongness and my wallet (good saddles are expensive), two features on error had me practically celebrating the moment. Shankar Vedantam, host of *Hidden Brain*, spoke in his podcast about the psychology of false beliefs. His interviews with researchers who study confirmation bias was one feature that initially nudged me into a little humbling self-reflection.

What is **confirmation bias**? It's our tendency to embrace data that supports what we already believe and reject information that doesn't confirm what we already believe. Vedantam said, "As we move through the world, quickly sifting through news headlines and the flow of information on social media, confirmation bias gives us a feeling of stability."

However, his guest Tali Sharot, author of *The Influential Mind*, added that confirmation bias "also means that it's really hard to change false beliefs. So if someone holds a belief very strongly, but it is a false belief, it's very hard to change it with data." As Vedantam explained, "We tend to accept information from people we trust, and once we do, we are resistant to changing our minds . . . Most of us think we arrive at our beliefs through logic and reason . . . [but] there are forces that may matter even more—our feelings, our social networks and our relationships with other people."

Regarding me, my horse, and the ill-fitting saddle, I really wanted to believe that my saddle would work and that Barry would be fine with it. Coming to terms with my wrongness was a process involving my acceptance of new information, which was delivered in a variety of gentle ways. It was a positive blend of reason and relationships. I also reckoned that my ego was interfering with what could have been a quicker, kinder conclusion about poor saddle fit.

*Being Wrong*, as mentioned earlier, is an intellectual romp of a book by Kathryn Schulz that also helped shift my perspective. She writes in her introduction, "I'm interested in error as an idea and as an experience: in how we think about being wrong and how we feel about it . . . In daily life, we use 'wrong' to refer to both error and iniquity: it is wrong to think that the earth is flat, and it is also wrong to push your little brother down the stairs."

Indeed, I had been feeling right about my old saddle and right about my being a good horse person; the two sentiments stuck together like glue. Humans, writes Schulz, "have a long history of associating error with evil—and, conversely, rightness with righteousness." I laughed when I read Schulz's words:

There is no experience of being wrong. There is an experience of realizing that we are wrong, of course . . . Recognizing our mistakes can be shocking, confusing, funny, embarrassing, traumatic, pleasurable, illuminating, and life-altering . . . But by definition, there can't be any particular feeling associated with simply being wrong. Indeed, the whole reason it's possible to be wrong is that, while it is happening, you are oblivious to it. When you are simply going about your business in a state you will later decide was delusional, you have no idea of it whatsoever. You are like the coyote in the Road Runner cartoons, after he has gone off the cliff but before he has looked down. Literally in his case and figuratively in yours, you are already in trouble when you feel like you're still on solid ground . . . It does feel like something to be wrong. It feels like being right.

Whatever falsehoods each of us currently believes are necessarily invisible to us. As soon as we know that we are wrong, we aren't wrong anymore, since to recognize a belief as false is to stop believing it. Thus we can only say, "I was wrong" . . . We can be wrong, or we can know it, but we can't do both at the same time.

Thankfully, I got over myself and started embracing what I was seeing and hearing from people I trust. In the end, with a new saddle on its way, the experience felt downright uplifting. The process was humiliating and illuminating at the same time.

## When Science Goes Sideways

If science were a horse, it would be an abused and neglected one. This horse would be taken advantage of and used as a vehicle to get humans where they want to go. It would be promoted as a Super Horse, treated like a vaudeville act, and leveraged to win an argument or make a sale—a sorry state for what should be a wonderfully valiant creature. No wonder media consumers have become so skeptical about science. Research has been reduced to sound bites and weaponized to serve the myopic self-interests of, in this case, the horse industry.

It was this recent post by Kentucky Equine Research (KER) that got my knickers in a twist: headlined "Radios and Gastric Ulcers: Is There a Connection?," the post by KER couldn't help but get readers thinking that there was indeed a connection, right? KER cited an Australian study that found that racehorses are more prone to ulcers if the barn radio is on. The horses do even worse if they are listening to talk radio as opposed to music. KER suggested buying their product RiteTrac for ulcer issues and perhaps turning off the radio.

The study was funded by the Australian government and conducted by Guy Lester, then an associate professor at Murdoch University, for the Rural Research Industries and Development Corporation. The goal of the 2008 project was to recognize and analyze risk factors for gastric ulcers in racehorses. Lester and his colleagues noted the following conclusions:

- City horses fare worse than country horses.
- Horses with turnout do better.
- Horses that spend time with other horses do better.
- The longer horses are in training, the more likely they are to develop an ulcer.
- Certain trainers have higher rates of horses with ulcers.
- Oh, and by the way, radio noise (which is more prevalent at those aforementioned city barns) seems to be a minor factor.

Can we be assured that the study's authors knew what they were doing and, in the words of Dr. Frans de Waal, "knew their subjects intimately" before studying them? Probably not. For instance, the authors acknowledge that horses got ulcers when taken in from turnout and stalled for seven days. But despite the widely acknowledged consensus on horses' need to move a lot and be with herd mates, they attribute the developed ulcers to altered feeding behavior, not the reduction in mobility and herd interaction.

The study was neither conclusive nor well designed, but it nonetheless had some salient points, which were, in turn, virtually ignored by KER. Because of people's interests in making money and serving their own, very human agenda, priorities get turned upside down. Bad practices are routinely justified. Rationales are put forward with conviction. All while the horses' best interests are swept under the rug.

What a shame if the outcome of this "research report" and the subsequent spread of it, like bad gossip, through social channels results in horse owners feeling good about their stalled horses because they've now turned off the radio or feeling okay about their chronically stressed horses because they've ordered RiteTrac. We can do better.

## Poor Things

Poor thing, 1: Like clockwork, scheduled with the turning of the leaves, I received two catalogs highlighting horse blankets. There were EasyMotion blankets, High Neck blankets, heavy-duty blankets, fleecy blankets, red, blue, plaid, and color-block blankets. There were consultants available, printed temperature guidelines, and multi-year guarantees.

These companies would like to convince us that we are straight-up bad, bad, bad horse owners if we don't order a blanket. Otherwise our horses are sure to suffer (suffer!) through winter. Better yet, we should order three or four: one for rain and cool temps, one for snow, wind, and colder temps, and a special one for the twice-a-year blizzard conditions. And don't forget the stretchy shoulder guard gizmos—they're like Under Armour tank tops for your horse to prevent rubs caused by, um, er, those very blankets you just shelled out for. Arghhhh!

Most horses do not benefit from blanketing and some may colic when the blanketing hinders their ability to take care of themselves. Horses have evolved to thermoregulate just fine. Just ask the wild horses who live long lives on the range. Just ask the tens of thousands of horses turned out to winter pasture in the western U.S. and left to "fend for themselves" until spring. Just ask my horses, aged 4 to 20, who do quite well in temperatures from -15°F to 95°F without my messing with them.

The key to their wellness is not our micromanaging their thermoregulation (which can go horribly wrong when an owner blankets on a mild, sunny day and virtually cooks the poor animal), but our offering adequate hay (undoubtedly more hay in the winter than during warmer months), freedom to move, and (less often than you'd think) shelter.

Poor thing, 2: In one of these aforementioned catalogs, I noted the tease: "Spooky Horse? Relax, we can help!" Since it's always interesting to learn about different training strategies for spooky horses, I thumbed immediately to the listed page. Ee-gads! It was a full two-page spread of supplements designed to calm your horse during "Spooky Season." I thought we called this time of year "autumn" or "fall." Who knew?

To paraphrase the selly-sell: Colder weather makes horses more "on edge." Buy something to chill them out. The pages feature a rider, crop in hand, pulling on the reins like she was hauling in a Gulf of Mexico marlin. The whites of her horse's eyes were visible and its tail was up. I felt bad for the fella.

Instead of helpful riding strategies—"if your horse wants to move, let him move but give him direction" or "let him graze and investigate his surroundings"—it was magnesium, tryptophan, inositol, chamomile, raspberry, chasteberry, and passionflower. I wanted to ask this company: Dude, like, when you gonna offer some reefer to me and my pony? Like, it would help us be one with the universe, man.

Here's what supplement companies don't tell you:

- There's no guarantee that what they say is in a given supplement is actually in there. Supplement outfits (for humans, dogs, horses, etc.) are notoriously unregulated.
- There's also no guarantee that supplements have any actual effect.
- Some supplements, when overdosed, can impact horses negatively.

Aside from adding selenium to a horse's diet in areas where there is a dearth of selenium in the soil (and therefore little selenium in hay and grass) and offering free-choice salt, research doesn't support this pricey habit. Let's challenge our brains, not our wallets. Let's solve our problems with real solutions, not sugar pills and consumerism-masquerading-as-do-goodism. The horses will thank us.

## Learning Schools and How to Avoid Tribalism

As owners and riders, it's vital to have an appreciation of how horses learn. We know they do not learn strictly by perking their heads up and following the direction of a human teacher. Like us, horses gain knowledge through a vast array of strategies. Some are intentional, like horse-human interactions. Some are more subconscious.

With help from "Understanding Learning: Theories and Critique," a chapter in *University Teaching in Focus*, edited by Lynne Hunt and Denise Chalmers, here is an overview. Keep in mind that although we've made great strides in understanding learning processes, which are the brain's ability to incorporate information and experience into memory and knowledge, this is a relatively new and constantly evolving field of study.

## Behaviorism

**Behaviorism** is the school of thought put forth by Ivan Pavlov and B. F. Skinner and is also thought of as learning by association. This type of learning involves behavior shaped and reinforced toward a target outcome (e.g., clicker training, pressure and release). It uses incentives, rewards, and penalties, and emphasizes an all-knowing teacher who controls the learning environment. Many of the following schools of thought argue that behaviorism is less about learning and more about rote performance of behaviors. Learning by association, they say, is one small, isolated element of the grand learning experience.

## Cognitive Science

This group of researchers believes that brains develop concepts, "flexible frameworks," on which we incorporate knowledge and experience. They study memory and attention and argue that learning is necessarily multifaceted. Cognitive scientists are interested in how the animal develops by maneuvering in the world, not just how it is able to recall and repeat requested behaviors. They study how subjects store, receive, and process information. How does a foal think differently than a mature horse? How does an isolated horse approach challenges differently than a horse kept in a herd?

Researchers in this field may define **intelligence** as "the success with which an individual selects, adapts to, and shapes the real-world environment by integrating various practical, analytical and creative skills."

## Neuroscience

This relatively new area of study considers the function of the brain in the learning process. We know, for instance, that the dopamine reward cycle can be tightly knitted into training sessions. We also know that dopamine release is boosted when there is greater uncertainty and greater unpredictability associated with the learning. Researchers have also found that the brain has mechanisms that allow learning to occur when errors are made (i.e., we learn from our mistakes) and that dwell time and practicing are natural parts of the learning process.

## Social Learning and Situated Learning

These researchers recognize the importance of social settings in animals' capacity to learn from each other and even from other species. Animals observe and copy behaviors. For example, horses learn where the watering hole is, and they learn to stand head-to-butt in order to tail-swish the flies away for each other. Undoubtedly, horses learn through their environment. Wild horses are reliably more agile than stall-bound horses because their surroundings provide often varied and challenging terrain. Domestic horses, meanwhile, adapt to motor-sensory input specific to human interactions.

Can we learn without following? As you might imagine, behaviorists, neuroscientists, and cognitive scientists have gotten pretty tribal as they adamantly subscribe to their particular way of thinking. A clicker training, or positive reinforcement, article I published years ago perfectly highlighted the divisive nature of discussions. Before long, there were dueling experts on both sides, touting their "truths."

But it doesn't need to be my way or the highway. I spoke with Curtis Moore, a horseman who wrote his master's thesis on the process of scientific mediation. As a community of horse owners and lifelong learners, he explained, we can build a framework of understanding that will make it easier to navigate these discussions *and* how we work with horses by being aware of the following:

- The biases of experts. Even the best science can be influenced by ulterior motives of funders or by subconscious or deliberate bias of the researchers.

- The error of positioning dueling experts on each side of the divide; it rarely results in greater understanding or discovery of common ground.

- The reality that some "junk science" (not peer-reviewed and/or funded by an entity with a vested interest in a particular outcome) is actually loaded with value judgments and only disguised as "science" to avoid the appearance of self-interest or ideology.

When it comes to moving forward with our horsemanship, it's good to consider a large body of knowledge and call out personal biases and political opinions. Groups like ours, Moore writes, can assemble three piles of study as we embark on a communal fact-finding mission: areas of agreement, areas of disagreement, and areas for which we need more information. Instead of a forced, black-and-white result ("Yes, clicker training is great" or "No, clicker training stinks"), we can find satisfaction in "Maybe." We can broaden our field of knowledge, for instance, by acknowledging clicker training as one of many ways in which we can communicate effectively with horses.

In this collaborative environment, we can strive to, as Moore says, "let opinion be formed by science instead of science being formed by opinion. The most valuable place we can be as horse people engaging with science is where we acknowledge that there are some things we know, some things that are always being refined, and that things are subject to change."

We are all essentially trying to get to the same place, where we're communicating effectively with horses. There may be different ways to achieve that goal. Civil conversations with other horse people whose views we don't necessarily share are an important way to advance our goals. Enjoy your horse work, talk with folks who have different opinions, and don't be afraid to get messy out there.

# CHAPTER THREE

# The Wisdom of WiseAssWallace

WiseAssWallace is a beloved guest columnist, aka my alter ego, at Cayuse Communications. From his pasture in southwestern Colorado, he's on a quest to improve horse-human connections and make lives better for his fellow equines.

## WiseAssWallace on Helmets

Dearest Humans, if there is one thing I envy of you, it's words. All day long, I talk with tail swishes, glances, feet placement, and ear position. Just once would I love to verbalize and share my inimitable wisdom. I was contemplating your wondrous mode of communication while letting the splendid words "panacea" and "panache" flow through my mind. Why were "panacea" and "panache" flowing through my mind? Let me tell you.

I watched this week as two riders took my pasture mates out of the paddock and proceeded to saddle up and ride. Or, shall I say, attempt to ride? In the first scenario, the human seemed agitated. I say this because it took her a few minutes to get a halter on my gelding friend, who is usually quite amicable. She then struggled with the saddle as well as the bridle. It seemed like she was rushing, though I didn't sense a storm or a predator in the area, so I'm not sure why she was agitated. My friend thought there must be a storm or a predator nearby, too, because of how this human was behaving. He started shifting around and getting worried.

I watched as they started riding. She reached for the gate, nearly lost her balance, and then accidentally spurred him. The weight shift and the dig to his flanks further worried my friend and he scooted forward, trying to make sense of it all and trying to get away from whatever the problem might be. To his great relief, she came off.

Other humans came running and there was a big commotion. I thought maybe there was a mountain lion in the barn or something. They gathered around the human and I heard one say, "Thank goodness you were wearing a helmet!" I learned what a helmet was by seeing them point to it. The rider even took it off and kissed it. It seemed that this plastic cap-with-strap was a veritable panacea for the humans. While we equines thought the whole incident was pretty messed up and scary, the humans seemed pleased at the outcome, thanks to this almighty cap-with-strap.

The second scenario was just as quizzical to me and my buddies. This cowboy, all dressed up with chaps, buckaroo boots, wild rag, and cowboy hat, came into the paddock to halter my equine associate. I watched as he proceeded to saddle her. There was something not quite right. Maybe he smelled fresh grass or was flustered by flies. I watched as he glanced in a window's reflection to check his outfit, and then walked past some girls playing with their ponies.

What he didn't notice was the balloons they were inflating. Nor did he notice the increasing irritability of my friend, his equine partner, as she heard these weird blowing sounds from the girls. I think she was fretful about leaving us, too, because she was tossing her head and whinnying in our general direction. The guy, full of panache and proud as a peacock, still didn't notice her anxiety and I'm thinking, "Oh, Lordy, here we go again."

He mounted up just as the girls let go of their fully inflated balloons. The ponies took off in all directions. The mare jumped sideways and spun, trying to get away from the commotion. The dude found himself in the dirt, watching from ground level as the girls giggled and ran after their ponies. He rubbed his head and wobbled as he collected himself and his hat. The fashionable cowboy looked better on the horse, but he just walked with her, and not in a straight line either. When he passed the reflection, he didn't look.

In closing, if I could speak to you, dearest humans, I would tell you that us equines don't know if you are wearing a helmet or not. We don't care if you are wearing a helmet or not. We do care if you are unbalanced, nervous, out of shape, and/or slow to react. We do care if you are distracted, preoccupied, or otherwise not aware of what's going on with us and with the moment. These are some elements of riding and partnership that we think you should be focused on. Check yourself. Or, as one of my favorites, Will Shakespeare would say, "The fool doth think he is wise, but the wise man knows himself to be a fool."

## WiseAssWallace on Colt-Starting Competitions

It's that time of year again, folks. Call it My Season of Discontent. Why? Because of colt-starting competitions, of course. Don't let them fool you into thinking this is a good deal for the horses. It ain't. What I see here is double shots of showmanship and ego with only a salt shake of actual horsemanship. *Show-off-manship* is more like it.

Even with good trainers in the mix, their work is soured, squandered, in fact, by the ill-witted incentive and misplaced motivation to git-'er-done with fireworks and fanfare. There's money and accolades for the human. What's in it for the horse? Nuthin' but confusion, stress, and a wholly horrible start. You might find these Highway to the Horse events entertaining, but let me present them from our equine perspective, in a way you might understand.

Consider, if you will, a trip to the dentist or driving on a four-lane highway in rush-hour traffic. You would not relish these experiences. Am I right? The dentist will put you in uncomfortable, vulnerable positions. Rush-hour driving will force you to make quick, stressful decisions. Good times, they are not.

Of course, these scenarios would be more manageable if you had some decent experiences leading up to them—like your mom takes you to a children's dentist with a cool aquarium in the waiting room, and when you sit in the chair at each visit, there's a television showing cartoons on the ceiling, bubble-gum-flavored fluoride, and a free toothbrush at the end. What a deal! Or like you spend time driving on gravel backroads, learning how to shift, brake, and turn with the summer breeze blowing through your hair, and then you get to practice going fast and passing on a two-lane state highway.

But noooo, colt-starting competitions aren't about proper preparation or building on good experiences. In fact, they are specifically geared to highlight the freak-outs us equines will inevitably have as we are put in sketchy, involuntary, and compromised positions. Believe me. I've had to counsel many a horse who's come to our pasture after being run through the gauntlet of a Highway to the Horse. They are damaged compadres, sorry to say. What else would you expect?

Again, consider our perspective. Take a fresh, young horse who's been hanging out with buddies, minding his own business, then put him under the lights, with frenetic crowds and loudspeakers. Dang, just this setup would set me on edge! But noooo, we're going to introduce you, Young Horse, to a human who aims to halter and saddle you in a matter of hours. Not shocking enough to the system? Let's see how you handle it when this human snaps bullwhips and stands up in the saddle. Having fun yet, Flicka?

Would you like a root canal on your very first dental visit? How would you manage that four-lane, rush-hour drive before you even have your license?

After they've been "started" like this, my pasture friends have issues. I call them Highway of the Horse Hangovers:

- They're shut down. They learned that if they submit, things will be easier. During the course of the event, they go from sweaty and worried to sweaty and listless. It takes a smart, kind, patient human to bring the life back in their mind and body.

- Their foundation is as fragile and frail as Little Piggy's stick house. When asked to step up and, say, be a productive ranch horse or a reliable trail horse, these equines either overreact or check out. It takes a smart, kind, patient human to rebuild their confidence and their mental and physical abilities.

So why not skip the next Highway to the Horse? There might be winners, but horses ain't among them. It might be fun, but not for us.

*WiseAssWallace would like to thank horsemen Amy Skinner, Kyla Strange, Steve Peters, and Mark Rashid for their input.*

# WiseAssWallace on Your Bad Arguments

WiseAssWallace has got himself in a twist over the advanced intelligence of humans. "For all their smarts," he says, "humans can sure get going down some brambly, ill-begotten paths. I'm talking nonsensical stuff, folks!" He had a little help from author Ali Almossawi and his book *An Illustrated Book of Bad Arguments*.

WiseAssWallace continues: Folks, unlike us equines, and for better or for worse, you are endowed with a developed frontal lobe. That means you have an ability to strategize and contemplate. You can romanticize and intellectualize, too. But can you pleeeaze use your brain in a way that doesn't embarrass yourself? C'mon, folks. Steer clear of bad arguments. They're like knotted manes, manure-covered coats, and untrimmed hooves. They make you look bad. Here are some simple examples of how you brainiacs got things back-ASSwards.

## *Argument from Consequences*

Explanation of Faultiness: Just because an argument leads to an unfavorable result, doesn't mean it's wrong.

Screwy Logic Example: Tie-downs (also known as martingales) are okay. I don't want to stop using one on my horse because then he'll throw his head all around. Besides, it won't look good.

WAW Wisdom: Using a tie-down can create insane brace and balance issues for your horse. It results in what Amy Skinner calls an "upside-down" horse. It'll take a long time to bring your horse back from such ill treatment, and your horse may indeed throw his head around with this new freedom. It will come down to better, lighter, more patient training on your part. As for "it won't look good"? Deal with it. Your horse will thank you.

## Appeal to Irrelevant Authority

Explanation of Faultiness: "An appeal to authority is an appeal to one's sense of modesty . . . which is to say, an appeal to the feeling that others are more knowledgeable," says Almossawi. Another version of this type of appeal is the appeal to ancient wisdom, "where something is assumed to be true just because it was believed to be true some time ago."

Screwy Logic Example: For generations, horsemen have given their horses grain to build muscle and stamina. So, it's good to give grain.

WAW Wisdom: Just because horsemen of yesteryear gave their horses grain, doesn't mean it was the best thing to do. And another thing: horses back then had vastly different lives than most horses do now. For starters, most were used many hours a day and were not kept in stalls. They may have needed extra calories that grain could provide, and they were at less risk for colic because they were moving a lot and, again, not kept in stalls.

## Not a Cause for a Cause

Explanation of Faultiness: This line of thought assumes a cause for an event when there is no evidence for it.

Screwy Logic Example: This week, I chewed raspberry-flavored bubble gum during all my rides. My horse was calm and agile every time. Therefore, my horse loves raspberry-flavored bubble gum.

WAW Wisdom: Your horse may have done better for any number of reasons. It could be that chewing gum distracts you from trail anxieties. It could be that chewing gum relaxes you and helps you to be a clearer communicator and better partner for your horse. You can love raspberry-flavored bubble gum for what it does to you. Have the awareness to appreciate how it modifies your movement and behavior.

## *Appeal to Fear/Slippery Slope*

Explanation of Faultiness: This erroneous line of reasoning describes a series of terrifying events that will occur as a result of accepting a proposition without clear causal links between these events.

Screwy Logic Example: We can't possibly put all our horses together. They will get rowdy and physical. They might get hurt. That'll be scary. We'll have to call a vet when one (or more!) of them gets hurt. That will be expensive. Therefore, our horses must be kept separately.

WAW Wisdom: It's true that horses can be physical and rowdy when they are first put together. But remember, horses are herd animals and benefit from being together. Research on the health and social benefits of group horse management is substantial. Whatever negative consequences your horses may experience at their initial group introduction will be outweighed by their improved well-being in the long run.

## *Hasty Generalization*

Explanation of Faultiness: It would be incorrect to form a conclusion "from a sample that is either too small or too special to be representative."

Screwy Logic Example: All my Facebook friends blanket their horses; therefore I can conclude that blanketing is proper winter horse care.

WAW Wisdom: Chances are good that your Facebook friends have a similar education, income, and cultural background as you do. Guess what? Five thousand Facebook friends can be similarly wrong. Social media is a crazy avenue for assessing best practices. The platform is set up for agreement and affirmation. If you're looking for answers to best practices questions, consider social media last.

## *Appeal to Ignorance*

Explanation of Faultiness: I don't know what it is, so it must be X. An appeal to ignorance is to assume a proposition to be true because there is no evidence that it is false. It confuses an absence of evidence as evidence of absence.

Screwy Logic Example: My horse can't canter. He never canters in the pasture with his pasture mates. When I ride him, he won't canter. When my friend rides him, he won't canter either. Therefore, he can't canter.

WAW Wisdom: Trust me, Silver can canter. He can gallop, too. Horses in the pasture are usually interested in conserving their energy. Cantering takes more energy than trotting, so unless he's particularly unsettled, he won't have a reason to move faster than a trot. As for not cantering under saddle, there are any number of reasons: It could be that you're not communicating well your request for a canter. Are you asking with your legs, but holding him back with your hands? Are you subconsciously afraid to go faster? Think about it, folks, but let your brain stay out of its own way. I'm WiseAssWallace and I guarantee it.

# PART II

Moving Toward Equanimity and Resilience

# CHAPTER FOUR

## A Conversation with Joe Morris

I met Joe Morris on a visit to the Paicines Ranch in Paicines, California, for the Rancher-to-Rancher (R2R) field day. Joe and his wife, Julie, run Morris Grassfed, a holistically managed cattle operation. He's also an R2R founding member.

When he was younger, Joe worked often with Tom and Bill Dorrance. He sought out Tom, driving over to nearby Merced, to seek his consult on more challenging horses. Bill helped him with roping. Over the years, Morris has excelled at horsemanship, stockmanship, and holistic management while growing his cattle operations in central coastal California. After my trip to Paicines, we spoke again by phone.

MADDY BUTCHER: Can you tell me a bit about how you got into working with horses?

JOE MORRIS: As a little kid I had a real affinity for horses, cattle, and the land. My grandfather, John J. Baumgartner Jr., was a really good vaquero. He had a real style like the vaqueros, and he was conscious of the value of that heritage; he taught me to value and love it, too.

When I was a boy, I never had to work too hard because he put me on good and broke horses. One horse, Doc's Whiz Kid, was a wonder. That horse, as the proverb goes, had forgotten more about working a cow than I had yet to learn. It was a thrill to go down the fence with him and turn back with the cow. I wanted to learn how to get that willing response from all my horses. Later, I read Ed Connell's book, the *Hackamore Reinsman*, and I started a few colts.

In 1984, I was 22, and I got up to the Spanish Ranch, which has hundreds of horses. Bryan Neubert had started there before . . . I was totally out of my depth, but I was still a pretty decent hand. I was given older quarter horse-Thoroughbred crosses to start. They were five to seven years old.

There was a small corral inside a barn, a 25-by-15-foot space that led into a bronco stall. I was dumb and didn't know better. It was kind of ugly. One horse, Matador, was mean, acted like he was proud cut. I asked my boss, Bill Kane, to help. Bill went into that space with him and the horse was firing at him with his hind feet. It was a death trap. He yelled to open the gate, and Matador went at him with his teeth and front feet. Nearly tore off the hinges. I did eventually get him started and ridden. That was the beginning of the magical world of horsemanship . . . I was not happy with this fairly brutal engagement with horses.

MB: Yes, that sounds less than ideal for both horses and humans. How did things progress for you?

JM: Around that time, Ray Hunt was holding a clinic nearby at the Van Norman ranch. I went to see him. Wow. I also was reading Tom's book, *True Unity*, and began having reasonable success. I ended up starting another 40 or so horses as I learned about this new approach. It felt good. It felt right.

In the late '80s and early '90s, I learned a lot more. I moved back to San Juan Bautista in 1991 and started visiting with Tom. He'd quit riding by then. I never saw him on a horse. I knew Bill as well. I loved Bill. He taught me a lot about roping. But I resonated more with Tom's way. Bill's pedagogy was a bit oppressive. He was trying to keep people out of trouble . . . But sometimes you need to get into trouble to learn. Tom allowed the struggle. I believe I'm not as good a learner as my horse.

Around then, I got the family brand, borrowed some money, and started ranching the family's 200 acres. I continued to learn from Ray, Tom, Bill, Allan Savory [founder of the renowned Savory Institute], and Bud Williams [pioneer of low stress stockmanship]. They all taught principles. It takes a lot to make principles your own. People can talk theory but have no feel of how to apply it. But that's the challenge.

MB: I'd love to hear any anecdotes from your time with Tom that you might like to share.

JM: Merced, California, is pretty hot in the summer. I was working with this horse, Rose. She was very high-strung, very sensitive. She was hard to catch and hard to do things with. Tom was watching her and said, "This is going to be a really good kids' horse," which seemed crazy to me. But, of course, she did turn out to be a great kids' horse. We still have her.

He was giving me suggestions and asking me to work with her in a certain way. He was suggesting doing serpentines, point-to-point, riding in a straight line, riding in a perfect circle. Riding straight and riding in perfect circles are simple but hard exercises. You need to be so mindful of horses' feet and mind. When relaxed, these things are possible. But you don't necessarily need to struggle or force it to work. If one is constrained, then you can't relax.

It was a sunny, hot afternoon. He was sitting in his golf cart, had his feet up on the dash, and I realized he was sound asleep. He was just not worried about Rose. Meanwhile, I was so worried. He taught in his sleep. He was that good. Tom's sleeping made me laugh. He showed me I could relax, that I can back off, that I can allow it to happen rather than try to make it happen. The difference was game-changing for me.

MB: Tell me more about what you held dear, working with Tom.

JM: Tom could make a game out of things. He'd be creative and fun. I was working with this horse and we were having trouble changing leads. Meanwhile, there was this burro who liked grain but was hard to catch. Tom suggested I use my horse to catch it, herd it, and so I'd be working my horse like a stock horse or a cutting horse. So, of course, we had to change leads. My horse was good at this game, and things became fun for me. I forgot about the lead changes, and the relationship with my horse improved.

Tom was so good at that. He always saw the silver lining. He looked for the silver lining. He built on it until the whole cloud was silver. The horse would then feel good and the person would, too. There wasn't a finish point. Every day was an opportunity to figure things out.

When Tom was visiting with the ranch boss Bill Kane, in Nevada, he would go out to find strays. They would be miles from headquarters. Tom would make a game of bringing them back. He would have all the black ones on one side and all the red ones on another. He would make play out of what some would resign themselves to as just hard work.

I know a bit about brain science, that brains are wired to notice threats. There is a bodily response to identifying threats. But Tom trained himself to look for opportunities, to take pause with threats and look for opportunities to emerge. That's why things became relaxed, fun, and a game. For others, those situations would be stressful and that would translate directly to the animals. They're so sensitive.

Tom isn't responsible for my way of being, but we were kindred spirits. He liked peacefulness, as do I. Tom helped me to understand how to translate my deeper desires into daily practice. I've been trying to do that in all areas of my life: holistic management, gospel, theology, philosophy. All have lined up to be who I am and to help me help others.

MB: Can you help me understand how these ideas interrelate and how Tom helped you incorporate deeper interests and passions into your routines? I understand you spent two years in Venezuela, living with a poor barrio in Caracas, while volunteering for a project run by the Catholic Church. I'm sure that has helped to inform your views on life and daily practices.

JM: Regarding translating deeper desires to daily practices, for example, the Gospel is all about relationships, to the land, to neighbors, to yourself. The result is peacefulness. We want to be happy, successful, and peaceful people. Jesus didn't say, "In this situation, you do $X, Y, Z$." He said, "Love your neighbor." One has to figure out how to do that given your $X, Y, Z$ situation. The Gospel is principles. In a similar way, I learned that I could create a lot of problems if I didn't have wisdom. Tom showed me ways to approach situations.

MB: I know you have been influenced by a lot of folks, not just the Dorrances. Can you tell me more about people who have influenced your path and growth as a rancher and as a person?

JM: As it concerns the management of big herds and our ability to do it, while achieving profit as well as high-quality ecological results, I learned principles from people like Alan Savory and Bud Williams.

Bud said if you go out and do what you want to do in a certain less-than-ideal way, you can create problems that are too big for you to handle. If you go out and do what you need to do, things will work out well in the end. You are accountable for figuring out what it is that needs to be done, given $X$, $Y$, $Z$. There's no one who can do it for you. If you do it right, everything could be easy. This is what great teachers do for us, they challenge us and point to our own agency as the means to deal with the challenges that come along.

MB: I learned that you manage an incredible amount of land and cattle with a few good hands, dogs, and some excellent strategies and planning. Can you tell me more about that?

JM: We manage 12,000 acres of central coast rangeland over four main management units of 600 head, 900 head, 420 head, and 500 head of cattle. The topography is rough, steep country with big canyons. My intention is to produce profit and enhance the land ecologically.

In order to allow for plants to capture sunlight and carbon dioxide, those animals have to be calm. It takes quite a bit of skill to manage those herds with one, two, maybe three people. Often we are working alone with a couple dogs. The only way to get it done is if the cows are happy doing it. And it needs to be done efficiently, for there are still only 24 hours in a day. If you are going to use low inputs of energy, high inputs of wisdom are often necessary to make gains, including profit.

MB: As logical as it seems, your game plan sounds out of the ordinary, or, I should say, extraordinary.

JM: Those skills are latent in a lot of good cowboys where "cowboy up" is the conventional way. When not handled well, the animals get sick. Fencing is ruined. Costs go up and profits go down. But it's beautiful if it's done well.

MB: Do you think there's a shift that ranchers are trying these methods that you've embraced for so long? And, speaking of the greater society, do you see any connected shift there?

JM: There's lots of evidence that people are dissatisfied with major societal paradigms, like, say, away from organized religion and toward mindfulness. There's a contemplative lifestyle in which people value direct experience rather than institutions showing the way.

Ranchers are asking and looking for alternative approaches, holistic management techniques, Ranching for Profit, managed intensive grazing. All those things are empowering people to figure out things on their own and within a community. All that is evidence of how people are looking for more organic, holistic approaches to produce joy in their lives.

There were observations I've had for a long time and some were prompted by Tom. At that time, I didn't know how my cowboying was connecting to the greater good of what I wanted to do. I spent years working with the poor in Venezuela. And I was a peace and justice activist. But I never felt good about what I was protesting.

I realized I could teach people more about peacefulness in a ring with a horse or on rangeland with cows than through protesting nuclear war or writing some kind of article on injustice. Maybe for me it's not one or the other; maybe I can do both. This was a conclusion I drew a long time ago.

# CHAPTER FIVE

## Lives with Horses

As part of the National Cowboy Poetry Gathering's celebration, I sat with Randy Rieman, Bryan Neubert, and Maria Lisa Eastman for a roundtable, discussing horses and riders today. What follows is research and consideration of where we've come and where we're going with our equine partners.

## Today's Horses Have It Better and Worse

What was it like for horses in this country 100 years ago? When it comes to how they'd want to be treated, my hunch is that they fared better and worse. Back then, Americans had lots of space and there were lots of horses, about one for every family (25 million horses for a human population of about 100 million).

Here are positive elements of their 1920s situation:

- Most had plenty of room to graze and hang out together.
- They were fit, used, and exercised often.
- They ate mostly grass and hay.

Here are some negative elements of their 1920s situation:

- Most horses were "broke." Many owners sought to dominate them. Some trained and treated them in a manner that we might consider cruel and inappropriate now.
- Injured or disabled horses were shot or otherwise disposed of.
- As beasts of burden, some suffered from neglect, mishandling, or abuse. Millions were used in battles and wars and subsequently suffered and died.
- There was lots of bad gear and use thereof. Equipment, including severe bits, martingales, tie downs, and other harsh gear, made life less than pleasant for horses. Behind the poor equipment, of course, was poor education. Some horses, I imagine, lived lives with their ears always back.

In the twenty-first century, horses' situations are dramatically different.

For starters, while the U.S. human population has mushroomed to about 360 million, the horse population has shriveled. Estimates for the American horse population vary from 5 to 10 million in recent years. Horse owners on average have three horses, so there are only a few million Americans who own horses now, less than 1 percent of the population. If that. Most horse owners are middle- to upper-class, college-educated women, according to one study. At least three-quarters of horses are used strictly for recreation.

## Are horses better off?

Gone, for the most part, is the practice of dominating and "breaking" horses. Instead, we've seen a gentling revolution over the past decades, in which owners are increasingly interested in developing a partnership with their equines. But there is still plenty of bad gear and poor use of it. Behind the poor equipment, of course, is poor education. Sound familiar?

## Most horses are better kept, but is that better?

Horses are now suburbanites. That's something that is less than ideal for them. Folks spend more money on their horses now, but there is less space and fewer jobs for them. They move less. Many are kept in stalls. Horses today are more often fed grain and managed in isolation. These elements undoubtedly make them more susceptible to a host of ailments including colic, obesity, laminitis, and other problems that come from not moving enough, being fed too much, and not being in an open, herdlike setting. In broad strokes, if we were to consider the negative elements of each era, we have gone from undercare to overcare. Neither is good for horses.

## What lies ahead for our equine partners?

At the moment, horses have this weird, conflicted, hybrid existence in our society: while the law and traditionalists classify them as livestock (intended to provide an asset or income), increasingly, people see them as pets.

The vast majority of horses are used recreationally. A billion-dollar industry supplies horse owners with largely worthless stuff—adornments, feed, and equipment—that horses don't need. More positive developments are horse rescues and therapeutic centers.

Now, they're beasts of being, not beasts of burden. Only a tiny fraction of them are used for the more traditional work, that is, ranch work, farm work, and military or mounted police work. Instead, as my friend Maria Lisa Eastman likes to say, horses have "new work." She uses horses at her facility, Rainhorse Equine Assisted Services. She told me it's more accurate to say that she "partners" with horses. It's the horses who are the therapists. Humans are just facilitators. It's impactful stuff. Connecting with horses can be a metaphor for life skills, she said. "Clients learn to be strong but soft. They learn about boundaries, standing one's ground, and being okay with saying 'No.'"

When we think of horses' future, we must consider the overwhelming majority of humans who have zero contact with *Equus caballus*. We know that as the world's population becomes increasingly urbanized, more and more humans are losing touch with nature in general. It's unhealthy. And for the horses, the situation threatens their species' perpetuity.

Richard Louv, who coined the term "nature-deficit disorder" and wrote *Our Wild Calling: How Connecting with Animals Can Transform Our Lives—and Save Theirs*, wrote: "For millennia, our species has waged war on nature, and our isolation and pathologies have only grown. Now it's time to make peace, as individuals and as a species. Our ways may be awkward and searching, but we must do this. We know empathy is more powerful than technology. It's possible to choose empathy over separation and superiority . . . There is an urgent need for humans to make space, share space, and get along with other species."

Because women make up the majority of horse owners, their/our actions will be key to this possible development and to the future of horses. That might be a good thing since women have good capacities for listening and nurturing. That might be a bad thing because women are often guilty of anthropomorphizing and substituting consumerism for what's really best for the horse.

As a horse advocate, I believe humans are responsible for the perpetuation of the species and its welfare over time. We know, for instance, that cortisol levels and heart rates go down for those humans in equine-assisted therapy programs. What about the cortisol levels of the horse? How will horses fare in their new jobs and livelihoods? In this day and age, when miniature horses are traveling in vans and riding elevators to visit patients in hospitals, when sport horses endure countless cruel treatments as part of their owners' cutthroat quests for competitive success, when most horses are ridden only occasionally and live suburban lives in isolation, can we trust ourselves to treat them as they'd like to be treated? Do laws need to be reformed? Should prospective horse owners be required to pass an exam?

I'm reminded of a conversation I had with a rancher friend. I was telling him about some really cute Aussiedoodle puppies I'd seen. "I feel sorry for them," Dan said. "How are they supposed to know what to love and what to know and what to do?" Like an abrupt one-rein stop, his comment pulled me up short. It rang true: dogs have been bred for specific purposes. They are considerably happier when allowed and nurtured to do what comes naturally to them.

Our challenge, moving forward in this world, will be to keep horses out of museums, to continue to supply purpose for them, and most of all, to do right by them.

## Ambivalent Forecast for Horses in the Next Century

When I'm asked to forecast the future of horses in the twenty-first century, I see partly cloudy skies. I think first of the wildly different stances people assume around horses in our lives, in our neighborhoods, and on our trails. I consider, for instance, the range of reactions to an op-ed I wrote for *High Country News* (*HCN*), which was subsequently republished by *Adventure*

*Journal* and other media outlets. On *HCN*, the comments were supportive and acknowledged the horse's place in outdoor recreation and in the history of the American outdoors. Meanwhile, on *Adventure Journal*'s site, readers' reactions could be summed up as "Get outta my way, old-timer. And take the manure with you."

I have news for my fellow riders out there: it's going to get worse. Getting horseback in big country might seem sexy and iconic as an idea, but on the ground, bikers and hikers don't like the poop or the sizeable foreignness of horses.

To make matters worse, we number increasingly fewer on today's public lands, when compared to runners, hikers, mountain bikers, and even electric bikers (ee-gads!). In public digital spaces (like Instagram, Facebook, etc.), we are an aging, underrepresented population, too. Back Country Horsemen, a national organization that boasts hundreds of chapters and works on scores of trail maintenance projects every year, doesn't even have an Instagram page (although some individual chapters do). Compare this silence to, say, the social media shout-outs and representation for hunters.

Recently, the Theodore Roosevelt Conservation Partnership, which has some 200,000 followers on Instagram and Facebook, shared news that Congress had issued legislation to invest in the future of hunting, addressing its declining participation. The post got thousands of "likes." Show me an initiative to address the declining participation in trail riding. Show me some nationwide equine organizations, non-profits or for-profits, that are effectively taking up this cause. Isn't riding on public lands as storied and worthy as hunting on public lands? Our lack of collective social media presence and collective enterprise will certainly contribute to our downfall.

Part of the problem is our niche-ness. I was talking with a Purina guy at the Equine Affaire in Massachusetts a few years back. Since I've spent lots of time with horses in Maine, Massachusetts, Ohio, Iowa, Montana, Utah, and Colorado, I wanted to know what he thought about the broad spectrum of horse keeping across the country. He laughed. "A woman in California once asked if I could suggest a good Thursday feed. Her horse was turned out 24/7. She checked on him once a week."

Meanwhile, plenty of suburban horses are managed more intensely. Riders sometimes don't ride outside arenas. Owners spend lots of time mucking stalls, blanketing and unblanketing, grooming, and feeding custom diets. Among my horse-owning friends in Colorado, no one does this. Is it any wonder we struggle to relate to one another?

Disconnects hurt our chance to unify over what might seem like common issues. Take open space access: In the Northeast, there is scant riding on public land because there is scant public land. But in the western U.S., vast swaths of states belong to everyone. Take welfare issues: Along with most of my fellow Colorado horse owners, I could be cited for how I keep my horses if I lived back East, where many states require at least three-sided shelters for any horse acreage. Groves of trees provide cover here.

How do we unite when our mindsets are so incongruent? We all love horses, but we have hugely different challenges, goals, expectations, incomes, abilities, and cultures. Sure, there are popular associations for rodeo, eventing, dressage, jumping, gymkana, vaulting, reining, and every breed under the sun. Car owners have these kind of niches, too, but they all still tend to have AAA for road service. Where is our AAA?

I'm excited about more folks discovering horses through therapy. Perhaps equine-assisted services will be a knight in shining armor for the future of horses in the twenty-first century. Perhaps. It's terrific that more and more health insurance companies cover equine therapy. Every day, new riders are being introduced to its powerful benefits at over 400 PATH centers and other facilities. Horse work like this is also an nice optic that helps attract men and women, young and old, able and disabled. Peripheral outfits like Heroes and Horses (a Montana operation that guides veterans with horses) and spa retreats with riding elements are having a good time of it, too. All kinds of groups are finding ways to introduce horses to the increasing number of urbanites.

Still, I worry for horses' future. Like my friend Dan, who felt sorry for

the Aussiedoodle puppies bred for cuteness, I wonder how human preroga-
tives will alter horses and horse keeping over time. Will most horses be draft
crosses—mild-mannered and able to carry the average overweight American? Will they be hypoallergenic? Alas, any semblance of a horse will still be
better than a robotic one, right?

## Riders: How Long Will We Be Relevant?

Like any other niche community, us horse owners and riders know what
we like. We gravitate to anyone or anything that speaks our language. We can
spot each other a mile away. In my neck of the woods, the "I get horseback"
uniform is long, well-fitted jeans with roughed up cuffs over cowboy or paddock boots; knife in jeans' pocket; ball cap, often with sunglasses perched on
lid; and long-sleeved snap shirt (tee or tank top if it's hot). Truck ownership
(half ton or larger), and an unlimited capacity for talking about our horses
and our horse life are common traits among us.

Of course, uniforms vary depending on what you're doing. Working
cowboys, English riders, trail riders, endurance riders all have their angles.
We are millions strong, divided amongst disciplines, united in passion. It's a
wonderful, diverse community. Our focus and intensity have awarded us with
scores of great organizations, brands, and gear dedicated to every conceiv-
able micro-interest within our community: miniature horses, OTTB rescues,
camping with horses, coon jumping mules, Sulphur mustangs, Breyer model
horse fans. You name it. The list is long.

Yet despite this vibrant ecosystem, here's one thing I know: increasingly, we are all losing our voice in greater conversational contexts. Our club-
by focus is distracting and detracting from the larger task of representing
ourselves in and among the tens of millions of non-horse owners. We love
looking in and encircling ourselves with like-minded folks. But like any other
niche community, we struggle with the less comfortable task of reaching
out. It's like avoiding creek crossing or galloping out: our discomfort with
discomfort makes us less ready and less relevant.

Have you noticed? When it comes to our relevance in conversations around public land, lifestyle, sports, and healthy activities, riding does not rate. Forget about rating, it isn't even recognized. The very word "riding" now refers to stepping up on a bike or motorcycle or wave. But riding a horse? What? A *New York Times* article suggested tennis as the best sport for a longer life despite the crystal clear (to us) evidence that what we do is waaaay better for the mind, body, and spirit. Even badminton was mentioned. Horse riding was not.

We're outside the conversation when it comes to outdoor recreation and access to public lands. We have expos and trade shows for our horse-specific interests, but associating with more mainstream communities is hard. I've tried to horse-talk with folks at the enormous and enormously influential Outdoor Retailer. Blink, polite smile, eyes glaze over. I've tried to start a conversation about trail riding with SHIFT, a conference "where conservation meets adventure." Blink, polite smile, eyes glaze over. Horse riding can mean "adventure travel" and "hunting and fishing" and "wilderness therapy" and "outdoor education," but we're nearly absent in these conversations.

While there are myriad groups and associations to join within the horse community, few of them reach beyond horse owners. And many of us don't connect our horse-owning and riding identity, passion, and dedication to non-horsey communities. Back Country Horsemen of America is a storied, service-minded organization that's aging and not staying particularly visible or current. Its social media presence is paltry. I'm familiar with our flaws because last weekend, mea culpa, I failed to reach outside my horsey circle. I meant to attend the local fundraiser for Mancos Trails, which services and promotes multiuse trails, but something came up and I bailed.

I was chatting with Kate Schade, owner and founder of Kate's Real Food, about the riding-in-the-greater-outdoors conversation. Kate knows that horse owners and riders tend to be educated, loyal, well-resourced consumers. They make good choices, like choosing one of her Tram Bars over a Snickers bar or being passionate about public access to open space and sharing the trail. For her, riders are on boards, bikes, *and* horses.

Don't get me wrong. Joining and advancing our niche circles is good work. But if we don't travel outside our comfortable spaces, the greater world will assume we don't care or matter.

## To Drift, Not to Push

Rancher-to-Rancher (R2R) is a network funded by the Regenerative Agriculture Foundation through the Soil Carbon Coalition, an organization dedicated to improving agriculture practices, or, as its website says, "advancing the practice and spreading awareness of the opportunity for turning atmospheric carbon into living landscapes and soil carbon." Sounds like heady stuff, but really, it's all about being smarter with land and animals.

I traveled to California to report on an R2R field day, an event to address drought resilience. It was held at the Paicines Ranch, 100 miles southeast of San Francisco, a bucolic 7,000 acres that sustains hundreds of head of cattle along with a vibrant ecosystem with over 200 species of birds in its fields, marshland, and among its shade trees. They're wholly dedicated to regenerative agriculture here. I caught up with Joe Morris, who, at the time of this reporting, ran the Paicines cattle operation and is a founding team member of R2R.

The field day started with coffee and small talk, followed by a round (literally, with everyone sitting in chairs around a circle) of introductions. Who attended? Mostly ranchers interested in improving their understanding of best practices and learning more about, for instance, intensive grazing with generous rest periods for their pastureland.

As the demonstrations got underway, I moved away from the group to visit with two working cowboys on hand, Buck Highberger and Isaac Moreno, who work for Joe Morris. They spend most of their days horseback and are responsible for many hundred head of cattle on different parcels across the county. The R2R demonstration involved moving some 600 head from one intensive grazing plot to another. I asked Buck and Isaac if they were ready to push the cattle. Buck said, "Well, we're going to drift 'em. Not push."

"Drift" was a new word in this context for me. It's the kind of language that represents new attitudes and philosophies I'm seeing in vast and varied circles of the agriculture community here in the West. I see paradigm shifts in everything from predator-livestock strategy and holistic management to best horse practices and even how we treat our fellow humans. More and more I'm seeing quiet stories that speak volumes, plant seeds, and spur conversation. People like Buck, men and women with land and livestock in their veins, folks off the social media/press release/marketing machine radar have been having some incredible shifts of heart, mind, and routine.

Sometimes the shifts are over a few seasons of contemplation (like what does and doesn't work in wolf and grizzly country). Sometimes it's generational (like "My father ran this land into the ground"). Rarely is it coerced by government or provoked by some progressive, bicoastal entity telling them how it should be done. The change is coming from private conversations amongst themselves, cowboys experimenting and contemplating their relationship with land and animals.

In the horse world, we talk about dwell time, that moment or week that we give a horse to relax and revisit training on their own terms. Buck mentioned "windshield time," time spent behind the wheel, hauling horses from one parcel to another. The Outside Circle Show (working cowboys performing music), founded by Justin Reichert and run by Reichert and Nicole Grady, is having some similar conversations around working cowboys and western identity.

At Paicines, Joe Morris recalled Tom Dorrance, the legendary horseman and a mentor of his who lived in nearby Salinas: "Tom said, 'Observe. Remember. Adapt.'" It was a reminder that every day, agriculturalists are learning lessons from what the land and animals (livestock as well as wildlife) tell them. It was nice, by the way, to see Steve Dorrance, Bill Dorrance's son and Tom's nephew, attend the field day.

A lot of people I talk with say ranchers and farmers fall into two easily identifiable camps—traditional/conservative or hippy/organic. But there is great nuance to agricultural life and those who live it. You can raise beef, eat hamburgers, chew tobacco, throw a rope, wear a cowboy hat, AND have some incredible insights on animals and land. You can be a recycling, vegan college graduate AND be insensitive to land and animals. Not only is there a broad spectrum of agriculturalists, these people often evolve and shift as they spend more years living with animals and the land, as they "observe, remember, and adapt." For this journalist, it's these nuances—like Buck's use of "drift" instead of "push"—that make work exciting.

# Chapter Six

# 2020 Challenges and Lessons

In 2020, the world's economies, governments, and health systems seemed to writhe as the coronavirus spread from China. Then, George Floyd was murdered by policeman Derek Chauvin and demonstrations erupted across the globe. Even in quiet southwestern Colorado, there were protests.

In the middle of these historical developments, the East Canyon Fire forced us (myself, horses, and dogs) to evacuate from our home for several days. While I shifted my "office" from the local public library to my friends' dining room, my intentions remained fixed: to bear witness and report. After three decades as a journalist, that's what felt right and natural and necessary.

At Cayuse Communications, we developed the Cayuse Corona Community, which featured dozens of accounts from horse owners across our readership. I also wrote for the *Colorado Sun* and other publications on life with horses during some trying times. Oh, and during this time, I moved my household to a small off-grid property. This chapter features selections across topics with a common theme of challenge and adaptation.

## Quarantine Absurdities

I think about death and how dying alone in a hospital is probably the WORST way to go. Thoughts on death were prompted by seeing a dog riding unconstrained on the back of a Harley. Really dumb to ask a dog to do that, if you ask me. But would its death be more horrible than, say, dying alone in a hospital?

Folks in southwest Colorado are getting antsy. Any unity ("Together, we'll get through it," etc.) seems tenuous and fraying. One's feeling about mask-wearing (and political affiliation, it seems) is worn, not on the sleeve, but with the mask. From my unscientific polling, the left of center and pro-government types wear masks religiously (even when alone in a car, a behavior I find amusing). Those right of center and anti-government types have shed the masks long ago (if they ever wore them) and complain vocally about the pandemic being a hoax and what's wrong with sick people dying anyway? They had it coming.

I miss regular mass at St. Rita's of Cascia in Mancos. The bells ring at noon each day, which is nice, but it makes me miss it even more. Should I channel the strategic, nearly immobile patience of a spider? Are spiders Buddhist? No, this tactic is not for me. Staying sane means being mobile, in mind and body. It's my essential work. Like so many other horse owners, I'm fortunate to live rurally and have options for "getting out." I am not limited to essential errands, nor must I stay within 200 yards of home. For Mother's Day, I took a fellow mom riding: two horses, two dogs, two gals on a warm, breezy, blissful morning. We stopped to let the horses graze and watch the dogs roll in the moist, vibrantly green grass.

Running, riding, hiking, yard work, and horse work have all kept me relatively buoyant. Spring is an intense time for plants and animals. Have you noticed? Everything's busy and busting out with new life or the prospect of new life. In one morning's course, I watched a magpie carry nest-building material and paused to see a coyote mousing and a tom turkey puffing up, all blue and red, for the ladies. The horses are nearly shed out and my chicks are becoming chickens who scamper through the day, searching for bugs and grass. I'd like to think they love their new digs, but do you think they consider it a containment area? A prison? A quarantine zone for eternity??

With my friend, artist Jody Chapel, I produced a pandemic T-shirt. It emphasizes the ruralness of life here and thanks essential workers on the back. Cow, horse, and fencing make for one big smiley face. The fencing might be hash marks, counting the days, depending on your inclination and interpretation.

## Pandemic Elsewhere

In early March 2020, I visited my son in Panama, where for more than a year he had been managing a guest lodge and farm in the picturesque village of El Valle de Antón. A few weeks later, the country had its first case of Covid-19, brought to Panama by a woman from Spain. The government promptly took massive measures to contain the virus. Here's a glimpse of pandemic life outside the United States.

My son Aidan writes: "March 24 was like a light switch. All these decrees came down from the federal government." Up to then, people were celebrating carnival. "The only message around the Corona virus was the occasional 'wash your hands.' During carnival, people jam-pack city squares and scream to get hosed down with water from on high. It's literally anti-social distancing. Then as soon as the Spanish lady showed up, the entire country seemed to shut off."

Within days, 90 percent of businesses were closed. The airport was closed to non-Panamanians. At last count, over 6,500 people in Panama had died of Covid-19 while there have been about 400,000 confirmed cases among a population of 4.2 million. Checkpoints in all municipalities were set up, and all essential workers were required to show special permits. Aidan spent days filing paperwork for the many essential employees, so they could travel to and from work. With the farm no longer providing fruit and vegetables to lodge clients, Aidan distributed baskets of the surplus to those needing food in El Valle. His pregnant partner sequestered at home.

One evening, he got a call from one of his employees. Biking to work, Miguel had been stopped at a checkpoint. The police hadn't accepted his permit and he was detained at the barracks. They told him that he could pay a $100 fine or be put to work for nine hours. From early morning to evening, he slaughtered chickens and prepped them for cooking. Other detained workers mucked stalls for the mounted unit. Aidan contacted the police supervisor to ask why Miguel's permit, which he had been using without issue for weeks, was rendered invalid. A new shift of out-of-town policemen had been working that day, the supervisor explained. They must have been ill-informed. No other explanation was given.

Men and women may only travel for essential errands within two-hour windows, on specific days, and always within their hometowns. Aidan can go to the local grocery store between 6:30 a.m. and 8:30 a.m. on Tuesdays, Thursdays, and Saturdays. The prohibition law, in effect since mid-March, has been slightly modified: one six-pack limit per store visit.

Recently, they've started a garden and bought some chicks. These transactions involved websites, WhatsApp back-and-forths, and boxed curbside pickups. Days can be hot and dull. And, as Aidan says, "It's a little depressing. There's a lot of second-guessing. Everything has to go through a filter: 'Can I do this during my window for going out?' Parks are closed so there is no open space to escape to. We are encouraged, mandated by the government to retreat even further into our own worlds."

## Of Whoopie Pies and Wilderness

Here's the thing about whoopie pies: They aren't that good. Never were.

The official Maine state treat is a century-old tradition with a similar shelf life. Made mostly of sugar, flour, lard, and cocoa, they live somewhere between a cookie and a cake and are decidedly not pies. They are ubiquitous at the checkout counters of small grocery stores in Maine, like the Levant Corner Store outside of Bangor. Thanks to my son, I received a delivery of these fist-sized, brown-and-white units from the Corner Store. Plastic-wrapped and slightly misshapen by the 3,000-mile journey, they brought me instant glee and satisfaction.

So as not to choke, one must consume whoopie pies with a beverage. Coffee or milk are best. I had mine with wine. After carefully unwrapping one, I sliced it in half, placed it on a plate, and ate it ceremoniously while sitting before the woodstove. I ate the second half and reminisced over the ingredients of an upbringing: Mudflats, blackflies, pot-holed backroads, deep woods, and ocean. Lobster, mussels, spudnuts (doughnuts made with potato flour), and whoopie pies.

Now there are pot-holed backroads, juniper, piñon, rattlers, and the long, clear vistas of the Western Slope. There is craft beer and venison stew. I live at 7,500 feet elevation, exactly 7,470 feet higher than my childhood home in Harpswell. The expanse of public land is the biggest appeal to life here. Within minutes, I'm out on it.

With my two dogs, I travel south toward a Bureau of Land Management parcel and hike a mile of fence line, hoping to come across an elk shed. (Deer and elk often drop their antlers when they hurdle fences.) I find none. On a sloping bench, there are doghouse-sized boulders that have, over eons, found themselves in the middle of meadows. We climb one and stop for some water and a pause. The La Plata Mountains are about 20 miles north and gleaming in white. New Mexico lies a few miles south. Around me, there are hundreds of square miles of public land, one small town, and a few thousand fellow quarantined humans.

I see no one as I move down a steep ravine, holding onto tiny branches of mountain mahogany and scrub oak to keep from falling. I spot elk and deer tracks, some coyote and perhaps those are bobcat prints. Being alone doesn't bother me. Like a lot of writers and trekkers, I crave it, honor it, and celebrate it. Being "isolated," however, feels different. The pandemic has addled my brain and altered my wilderness experience.

I was watching *Harry Potter and the Order of the Phoenix.* (Like whoopie pies, *Harry Potter* is perfect pandemic fodder.) At the 67th minute, Hermione is describing Cho's feelings after kissing Harry: She's feeling very sad, because of Cedric dying, confused because she liked Cedric and now she likes Harry. She's feeling guilty, thinking it's an insult to Cedric's memory to be kissing Harry at all, and she'll be worrying about what everyone else might say about her if she starts going out with Harry—all very mixed up and painful. Oh, and she's afraid she's going to be thrown off the Ravenclaw Quidditch team because she's been flying so badly. Ron says, "One person can't feel all that at once, they'd explode!" Exactly!

My cerebral gyrations: I'm glad to talk more often with family and friends, but sad to not be with them. I'm struggling to adjust to the new communication routine. Am I calling too much? Not enough? I'm grateful to have horses and dogs, and happy to get out with them. I'm fortunate to have a healthy brain with which to think critically, to be observant, and to write. And I'm rattled that I cannot keep anything straight—from my toothbrush to my appointments to this essay. One person can't feel all that at once, they'd explode! My mind graciously augmented the whoopie pie moment. Thank you. Then it infected my wilderness time. Dammit.

I talked with my friend Chris, a fellow writer and adventurer. He sounded equally weary and frustrated. At home in California, he was struggling to get any work done or get anything done, period. "Pandemic? How 'bout pan-dumb-ic?" he said.

With horses, it's easier to function and focus. If you don't leave stuff at the door, your lack of presence will wreck your ride. If you're too distracted to realize it, your horse will let you know. It's harder when there is no thousand-pound animal moving and breathing beneath you. When not horseback, how to better soak in the expanse of my nearby Menefee Mountain and stop the seepage of pandemic preoccupations? Lately and quizzically, I'm calmer about things I cannot control, like the economy and public health. I'm less calm about things I can control, like my mental well-being. I view my own mind suspiciously as it alternates between arch adversary and consoler-in-chief. Be kind to yourself, I say.

And yet, in a dream, I am on a sidewalk, waiting to enter the grocery store. I stand six feet behind one person and six feet in front of another. Abruptly, a big, hairy hand enters the frame, grasping a giant rubber stamp. It is pressed down on the scene and leaves the inked date: December 1. I woke up. It was indeed still springtime. But I guess I should prepare for a long pandemic haul. Tell me it ain't so.

## Oranges and Lemons

Do you take the oranges? Outside my closed, local gym, there sits a box of oranges and lemons. The sign, scribbled in pen on a flap of the cardboard, says, "Virus-free fruit. Help yourself." There's a plastic bag containing other plastic bags. Another message that says, "If you are taking the last of them, please throw away the box."

Like many decisions nowadays, this one is more fraught than it might have been last year. What might have been a simple thumbs up or down is now a long-winded, circuitous debate that my brain has with itself. It's a roundtable discussion. Enabled by the outbreak, nurtured by the ensuing isolation, the inner talks are increasingly frequent, frantic, and freakish. Personal risk management, faith in community, love for humanity, resistance to disease, paranoia, and the taste of fresh-squeezed orange juice, among other concerns, are discussed at random and at length. The conversation is a baggage carousel. The viewpoints are bags. Around they go.

For the first few weeks of the pandemic, when social distancing was a new thing that officials stood behind podiums to define, I smiled at the implementation and optics of the policy here in southwestern Colorado. In Montezuma County, there are 26,000 people over 2,000 square miles. That's about a dozen people per square mile. One can be hard-pressed not to be socially distant. With about a dozen others, I live on a four-mile, dead-end, dirt road. We see each other rarely, mostly when we drive past and wave. Town is nine miles away. Now that the gym and the library are closed, my already limited interactions with fellow humans are at Pete Loyd's grocery store and the post office.

On the surface, life has not changed dramatically. Alone, I write and edit. I work online. I tend to horses and dogs. I eat and exercise. But beneath the surface, I'm preoccupied with the health and well-being of family and friends. I noodle over my finances, the future, and the future of my finances. While my hikes used to be silent and welcome reprieves from a day's busyness, I now fill them with phone conversations. When I'm with my horses, I'm struggling to be really there. With all my writing and publishing around how "*now is the perfect time to embrace your horses*," to ride, groom, and hug your horses, I'm hyper-aware and self-conscious. Look at me, spending time with my wonderfully therapeutic horses, my brain says.

And around the carousel we go: Relax. Focus on your horsemanship. Get softer with your nervous horse, Barry . . . But there's a veritable pandemic going on! I couldn't fly to see my kids if I tried. The end is nigh! . . . Spring is coming. Look at the grass coming up . . . F*ck the grass. When the horses are turned loose, to roam freely in the post-pandemic apocalypse, the new pasture grass won't matter . . . Maybe I'll check my phone again . . . Barry is waiting and watching. He's bobbing his head lower. He's relaxing . . . If only I could be more horse and less human. I get headaches, probably because I spend too much time using my phone, scrolling Instagram, texting, checking emails. It's bad for posture, eyes, and peace of mind. Screen time has been creeping up to more than three hours a day. The aforementioned phone tells me.

To shake it off, I dedicate Sunday to carpentry. It would not be a few hours of distraction, chipping away at the long to-do list. It would be a whole day of mud, cold weather, and physical labor dedicated to constructing a custom, homemade chicken coop. (Yes, like so many others, I have darling, weeks-old pullets who will soon need a place to live and lay.)

Some time ago, as a single mom, I worked in the trades, swinging a hammer and wielding power tools. I learned to dig postholes, build walls, floors, shelves, and rivet a roof. I'm constructing the coop completely with used materials, mostly from a rotting gazebo I disassembled last summer and from old pasture fencing and fixtures. The pièce de résistance? The hens' door, complete with smooth-moving hinge and raccoon-proof fastener. The hinge is from an old pasture gate. It is massive, galvanized, triangular, and covers most of the 12-inch door's width. I am calling it the *Game of Thrones* door.

The end of the day comes quickly. As the sun sets, I sit on the porch and drink a beer. I watch my dog Monty, as he watches the horses. Later, I walk the road in the dark and feel snowflakes on my face. Still later, I sit near the woodstove and make a round of calls to family. No headache. I took some oranges and lemons. The fresh-squeezed juice and tea with lemon and honey were novel and delightful. Tomorrow, I'll make lemon squares or maybe lemonade.

# Wildfire Evacuation: No Time to Think

Last Sunday was like most others. After a lazy breakfast of tea and toast, I was ticking off my property project list. In the late morning, I gathered equipment—loppers, bug dope, and two quarts of water for myself and the dogs—for trail clearing east of my home. It was pleasantly hot and breezy.

I call this trail the Lollipop Loop: It heads east, up a draw that's thick with scrub oak, aspen, ponderosa pine, and Douglas fir. The draw rises steeply on each side, from 7,500 feet to over 8,000. After a quarter mile, it forks, heading southeast and northeast. Head southeast and you'll find my loop trail climbing 500 feet and crossing a ridge before dropping down to pick up the northeast gully. The path is lollipop-shaped, fun, rough going, and takes only a season to become overgrown and in need of trail clearing yet again.

After two sweaty hours, I'd run out of water and energy and was working my way back home, picking up cut branches and tossing them off the path. As I crossed the pasture and got back into cell service range, my phone rang. It was my friend Wayne, who yelled through the line, "Maddy, there's a fire in the canyon!"

"What fire?" Like a cartoon figure, I stopped, pivoted, and cast my eyes on an enormous column of smoke. It had been billowing just hundreds of yards from where I'd been clearing trail. Deep in the gully, with the fire above me on the ridge, I had been happily oblivious. Now, I was charged. I called another friend, ran to the garage, dropped my gear, and engaged my plan.

Plans actually go against my nature. Self-employed and spontaneous, a run, a ride, a social detour, or one of many property projects often interrupt my schedule. In fact, I stopped calling things "interruptions" and "schedules" a long time ago. But for this dire moment, here in wildfire country, during a drought, with the scars of the massive 2012 Weber Fire just across the road, I had a plan and moved quickly.

I called the dogs and raced into the house. I moved to the spare bedroom, grabbed my folder of essential documents, and put them in a suitcase.

I left the dogs in the house, grabbed a water bottle, and paused to compose myself and my to-do list: hook up trailer; grab two bales hay, dog food, and water; add change of clothes to suitcase; take phone, laptop, and chargers for phone and laptop; breathe.

Two friends arrived within minutes. My horses were haltered and loaded within a few more minutes. Dogs and suitcase loaded in a few more minutes. My phone started ringing and buzzing with texts and calls from friends and neighbors, who like me, received the rapid and repeated county emergency management text messages about the East Canyon Fire and this area's mandatory evacuation. From Lollipop to Loaded in no time.

For years, I have reported on the need to be prepared. As a newspaper reporter, I covered wildfires and interviewed firefighters and civilians. Never have I been an evacuee and had the logistical and adrenaline challenge that go with evacuation. This week, I learned the importance of three things:

- **A practiced plan.** Our community has advocated for preparedness and done mock evacuations. I hooked up my trailer and grabbed my essentials quickly and with no fuss. My horses loaded quickly and with no fuss. These were elements I've deliberately practiced.

- **A connection with government and emergency personnel.** Text messages and emails from the county emergency management agency were extremely valuable. Neighborhood communiques were fabulous, too.

- **A reliable social network.** I live alone and could have managed alright. But my friends were superstars. They arrived immediately, managed all needy, niggly bits—from animals to watering left-behind garden to grabbing additional socks and underwear. Other friends offered places to stay for me and my animals. Cold beer, burgers, and wiseass conversation —otherwise known as soothing balms in times like these.

The fire has grown from an initial lightning strike to 3,000 acres in a few days and has brought in VLATs (Very Large Air Tankers) dropping slurry, helicopters with water buckets, and engine companies from across the country. It is a Type 2 fire, which is an indication of its complexity (involving structures in challenging terrain) and its size.

My neighbors and I are grateful to the firefighters and to our collective fire mitigation work over the years (supported by folks like Wildfire Adapted Partnership and local fire officials). Both elements have meant that no lives or structures have been lost. Safety has been the steady focus. Fingers crossed, I'll get back to my trails, hikes, rides, wildlife watching, and the spontaneous joys in the backcountry sometime soon.

## A Pasture Moment

Some months back, I was riding my big project horse, Barry ("project" because we've got stuff to work on and "big" because he's 16½ hands). We'd moved up and down through the gaits and had had a lovely two-hour trail ride. Returning home, I grabbed a water bottle I'd left on a fence post at the end of the driveway. He spooked and bolted, something I wrote about in the discussion on the "Hot-Cold Empathy Gap." I did not succeed in slowing him down and came off hard, at a gallop, about 100 yards down the road. We collected ourselves. I stepped back into the saddle, and we rode for another 30 minutes.

This spring, we picked up where we'd left off. Things were fine, but edgy. He was nervous and I was nervous. One night, I was hanging out in the pasture, drinking a beer, and watching him as he watched me. Why push? There had to be a better strategy.

My new plan was not so much a plan but an acknowledgment that pushing was pointless. Mmm, maybe not pointless since the intention was progress. But we were missing each other, looking past each other at things we valued more—for me, it was riding; for Barry, it was safety. I'd skipped by opportunities for connection and growth.

So, for months, Barry and I have been having a redo. Learning about equine bodywork has helped me help him. "Don't touch my poll!" has always been his mantra (from what I suspect was years of mishandling). So, our nightly sessions are mostly about touching the top of his head, rubbing it, massaging it. He gets ear strokes and neck flexion. There are long, uninterrupted sessions of licking and chewing and yawning. Sometimes, he rests his chin in the crook of my elbow or on my shoulder. His breathing is slow and regular. When I unhalter him, he often stays with me. It's not riding, but it is progress.

"What happened? What can I do for you?" are questions I try to ask more often, not just for Barry but in general. While many are directly affected by the chaotic tragedy of Covid-19, more of us are just inconvenienced and isolated. We have time to bear witness, to look out and look in. Has the pandemic helped us white folk to finally see blistering inequalities in government and society? Were we ready to be riled because Covid-19 primed the pump? I'd say so.

## A Driveway Moment

I was changing a tire in the driveway. I'd jacked it up and removed the flat. Then I listened as the driveway started making the faintest of gravelly noises. I watched as the jack tipped ever so slowly. But not that slowly. Faster than a tree falling. Slower than dominos.

I'd parked the car on a bit of an incline and had not set the emergency brake. I can't remember why this didn't seem important at the time. I cursed and rushed to get something, anything, to put under the axel. I placed a concrete block there and realized it was too low, that the wheel would still hit the ground when the jack collapsed. The dogs looked on as I ran for another block. The jack gave way just as I wedged the second block on top of the first. Sometimes it feels like the moment gives us a moment to right the wrong.

This summer, in rural southwestern Colorado, periods of ho-hum, git-'er-done routines are pocked with bouts of reckoning. Long, sunny days with a chance of thunderstorms. I'm not sleeping well. It's been hard to write.

Distractions are myriad. While writing is difficult, I continue to believe that it is my best vehicle for bearing witness. Yet so many humans are fairly flagellating with reflection and opinion and sharing and pontificating. Is my voice valuable? Is this exercise pointless?

Body and brain struggle with sessions of sitting. It ain't cutting wood, or running four miles, or reviewing a new product, or producing a newsletter, or massaging a poll, or riding a mustang. And yet. Converting synapses to sentences feels powerful, painful, necessary, pleasurable, indulgent, challenging, and full of agency. It's complicated. But it's not like there aren't other things to do. What is worthwhile nowadays anyway?

I was talking with my son Cormick, who is isolating and working from home in Washington, DC, and who I haven't seen since March. He said that in order to write well and true, writers shouldn't expect their pursuit to result in happiness. Writing does, however, give meaning to our notions of freedom and to our place in the universe. So there's that. Humans have long felt distinct from nature by virtue (and, boy, that's a loaded word in these times) of our frontal lobes and our consciousness. But if the pandemic has shown us anything, it's revealed that we, too, are part of the natural world.

## A Ridge Moment

I get up on the ridge, east of my home, to view the desolation of the East Canyon Fire, which turned 3,000 acres to ash and had our neighborhood evacuated for five days. The scrub oak, the juniper, the piñon, the ponderosa, the mule's ears, and the yucca. All gone. Lacking flora, there is no fauna. Lacking flora and fauna, there is no noise. I squat on a rock, overlooking the vast burn area. I'm mesmerized and alone and relishing the silence.

When I climb the ridge a week later, green shoots are popping up. In another week, despite the heat and lack of rain, it's greener still and I'm reminded that with devastation comes the chance for renewal. I'm adopting an understanding of links: Running the ridge supports the writing; writing nurtures my soul and connects with readers; massaging Barry's poll makes us better partners; wildfires and pandemics can reveal our errors and give us a chance to right wrongs; a tree is not just a tree, but part of a vast network that includes microbes; microbes are germs. Does that touch a chord?

The East Canyon Fire was just another 3,000-acre fire of the 2020 season. No lives and nary a structure lost—just a blink in the long, smoky wince of 31,000 fires and more than 2 million acres burned. But suddenly, on a hot and breezy Sunday, dozens of us were heeding mandatory evacuation orders. Later that day and for days after, we watched as DC-10s dropped red streaks of slurry on the ridge, as 400 firefighters made busy our dead-end gravel roads, as helicopter pilots deftly dipped buckets into the canyon's two tiny ponds. Within two weeks, the fire was officially out, and I got up on the ridge to consider the devastation.

It was awesome. I mean that like the dictionary says: "Inspiring reverence, respect, dread, and wonder." What captivated me the most was the game trails. They were revealed, like inscriptions on paper rubbed with charcoal. Ghost paths of routine journeys traced. Oh, the stories they told. In another week, green shoots of oak and yucca would sprout. We'd see fresh deer tracks and birds flitting, and we'd be reminded that devastation is but a prelude to renewal.

## Pressure and Release

Someone sent me a playlist of dance songs this morning. By eight o'clock, with two cups of tea in me, I was dancing around the kitchen and living room, feeling relaxed and free of cares. The dogs watched. "Who is this woman?"

It was different from that night last week when I hit a nadir of pandemic angst. When you reach this moment—I'm guessing most readers have— would you actually call it a low point (nadir) or a high point? Would you celebrate having it behind you, like you would a summit, trotting downhill in relative glee? Or would you rejoice as if you were climbing out of an abandoned mine shaft, happy to see the sunlight after a lengthy, foreboding dark? If memory serves (a legitimate concern nowadays), it was as close as I've come to losing my sh*t. And, to boot, I almost burned down my house.

It was, in fact, a foreboding dark that kick-started the angst. I had just returned from the 34-mile roundtrip to town. For most of the day, it had been snowing and the roads were bad. We (the dogs and I) went creepy-crawly, 30 miles an hour, on the state highway where folks usually travel twice as fast. The light was so flat, the snow so steady, and the wind so wild that for the last few miles home I could not tell the road from the not-road. Trees and telephone poles helped. I held fast to the steering wheel, ready to sense the possible dip into the borrow ditch.

Safely home and squinting into sideways-snow, I rushed to get chores done before darkness fell. The horses were hungry and skittish. Even when I placed their hay in the shelter, the wind churned it around, further unsettling them. I stomped on the ice in the water trough. The temperature was dropping with each minute.

The chickens—my three darling laying hens, which, like so many others, were acquired as wee chicks this pandemic spring—had their shoulders hunched up (the universal pose for feeling frigid, it seems) and were already roosting. This would be the coldest night so far this winter, getting to just below zero Fahrenheit, and, therefore, it would be the coldest night they'd ever experienced. Would they be okay? Are chickens, born in some Arkansas warehouse and shipped to Big R's across the West, bred and ready for Colorado winters? If they freeze to death, would I have the courage and skill to "get closer to my food" and harvest them as meat hens?

It would be better if they lived. I heated a big pot of water, secured its lid, and placed it in the coop. It'd be like a hot water bottle taken to bed, right? Maybe this would keep them from freezing. (For the record, I ruled out a heat lamp because of a stark childhood memory of a coop, birds included, caught afire by one. Or, at least, that's what I recall, if memory serves.) I closed the coop door and headed inside.

This is my first winter living off-grid. I have solar panels that generate electricity for the house and a woodstove for heat. My closest neighbors are more than a half mile away. They have curtains on all their windows and occasionally I can hear them yelling at each other. The National Forest is, in fact, my closest neighbor. I visit it every day for long runs and rides. Sagebrush, grasses, piñon, and juniper cover the open, rolling hills. I can see south to New Mexico and west to Utah.

I stoke the fire and make dinner. To share some virtual cheer and a beer, I call my friend in California. Chris tells me about having to put down his dog yesterday. He talks about how wretched the procedure was, and how great a companion she was for 12 years. I cry when he tells me about her last trip to the beach, about her eating cat food, and about her having puppy-esque energy well into her senior years. "I was just hoping 2020 didn't take her, too . . ." His voice trails off.

After I hang up, I can hear the wind anew. It's rattling the deer and moose antlers that I fixed to the side of the house. It's shaking the dryer vent and the hardware-store thermometer that I bought as a housewarming gift to myself. The house whistles and moans. Have you noticed that anxiety often happens when you have small, immediate, solvable worries that get pig-piled by bigger, less tangible, less solvable worries?

Small immediate worries are things like frozen chickens, cold horses, and a cold house. These get jumbled among bigger intangible worries: Will my parents in Maine be okay this winter? How is isolation affecting their well-being? When will I be able to see them again?

What defines a good safety net? Is a safety net savings and resources, or is it support of family and friends and a sense of well-being? Am I losing it? What is "it"?

On the drive to town earlier, I saw three people walking on the other side of the highway. They were togged up in jean jackets and weird hats and were leaning into the wind. One of them was pushing a walker through the snow. As I drove past, a big highway truck, equipped with a front plow and a wing plow, was headed toward them, fanning great curtains of snow. Would they be okay? Why do I circle around and around a namby-pamby internal struggle when there are folks struggling to stay standing? What matters? Or, equally confounding: What matters more? "Stay positive and productive," my mind implores. "Shut up already," I answer.

I empty hot coals into the ash bin and reload the stove with logs of scrub oak that I cut last year. I set the bin outside and check the chickens (still alive) and horses (still on high alert) and break the ice in the water trough again.

To keep an eye on the fire and to feed it during the night, I decide to sleep on the couch. The dogs are antsy with this new sleeping situation. Monty starts beside me on the rug, then stares at Peeko until she relents and gives up the better dog bed. Peeko repositions herself on the lesser dog bed. The wind blows and blows. I worry about the chickens, the horses, the parents, the highway walkers, and myself. It seems there is nothing to make me feel better and no one to tell me "just breathe."

Morning comes after the fitful night. Before tea, I bundle up and head out to check the animals and run the dogs. It's calm, sunny, and everyone is fine. But the thermometer has been blown clear off its tiny hinges, and, what's worse, the nighttime gale tipped over the ash bin. Hot coals melted clear through the decking, leaving a fist-sized hole. If I had been just a little bit dumber, if the ash bin had been just a little closer to the house, if the wind had been just a little bit more northerly, if the decking had been wood not plastic, those coals might have set the house afire.

In my mind, someone says "by the grace of God." I shake my head, take a breath, and eke out a smile. I walk around the house to the mudroom door. There, on the stoop, with no note or clue as to its deliverer, is a six-pound, "party size" red-and-black box of Stouffer's lasagna. Left by neighbors? Will wonders ever cease?

## Brace, Panic, and the Long Journey to Relaxation

I fell over. During the holidays, I navigated through Covid screenings, six hours of flying, multiple security and customs clearances, three police checkpoints, and ten hours of driving to meet my family in Panama. It was late evening when I arrived, at last, in Cambutal, a small village of about 600 people on the Pacific coast.

Inside our rented cottage, I met for the first time my new granddaughter, Aila Lucia, born in August. I held her with wonder, admired her chubby arms, her deep brown eyes, and eventually handed her back to her father, my eldest son. It was way past her bedtime. Perched on the arm of the couch, I took in the sublime scene of my three sons, their partners, and the next generation. They were laughing and late-night chatting in Spanish and English. I fell off the couch and onto the floor. What just happened?

It was a brief disconnect between a relaxing body and a yet-to-relax brain. Or, maybe vice versa. It was funny as hell and had me considering how mind, brain, and body can work with and against each other, depending on the individual and depending on the moment—like distinct players in the game of living. I recovered quickly from my couch crash, with laughs and a solid night's sleep. Over the next few days, we rocked in hammocks, drank coffee, ate good food, and most of all, headed to the beach for swimming and surfing.

I don't surf. With some scary water-related incidents in my past, I struggle whenever things feel even slightly out of my control. In Panama, I started getting panicky when waves were knocking me down. My son Beau kayaks and surfs with dedication and zeal. He's an accomplished whitewater paddler and has been surfing Maine waves this winter. It wasn't surprising that his approach to water—and to scary things in general—was drastically different than mine.

On a regular basis, his way to calm led from his body to his brain, not the other way around. It was not an intellectual exercise. It was practiced intuition that one sees frequently in extreme athletes. "You start by relaxing one part of the body. Like closing your eyes and relaxing your head and neck. You can acknowledge that it feels more comfortable than the alternative. Eventually, it gets easier being in stressful situations," he told me.

Since he was a teenager, Beau has honed this technique. He learned from watching more experienced kayakers. When faced with activities that might bring on panic, he didn't like the feeling of tightening up. Feeding off negative emotions of struggle and panic didn't work. He'd get worn out and stressed. Instead, he practiced relaxing. "I can fall into the flow. Ultimately, the waves are bigger than you. The rapids are stronger. The only way to get through is by relaxing," he said. "Everything I know about panicking is that it gets you nowhere."

I have work to do. As a 56-year-old, my behavioral patterns—good or bad—are like well-worn cobblestones. The territory ahead, neurologically speaking, involves bushwhacking new paths and resisting the old avenues. Flow seems elusive. Relaxing when things are out of my control: Is that possible?

My project horse, Barry, may have a similar journey. His past mistreatment and poor trainer history manifests in braced necks and shoulders. I've been working with Amy Skinner to create a safer, more enjoyable, more relaxed existence for him. I expect this will help him become a safer, more relaxed, more enjoyable riding partner. As we exchanged videos, Amy explained her strategy: In essence, the body can be trapped by the brain's set patterns. The one-time brace of years ago has become an auto-brace. We want to unlock the physical patterns that are tied to the brain's wiring. We are working to undo the auto-brace through new movement.

One exercise involves rubbing his tight neck while leading at a walk. In this way, he can eventually feel how much better it is to walk without a brace. Over many sessions, Barry is learning that a lowered head and a relaxed neck feel better than the alternative. Like Beau's strategy, it is almost counterintuitive: Change the body to change the brain. Introduce new movement to effect changes in neurological patterns. A trickle-up approach.

Since we were enjoying some success in the paddock, I decided to take Barry out on the trails. I rode my mare, Shea, and led Barry over five miles of backcountry. Afterwards, I reported back to Amy. I was dismayed:

Barry was a nervous wreck. He held his head high and startled at nearly everything. Only a few times did he lower his head. He did it once when I rubbed his neck; he lowered his head, gave a deep breath out, and licked and chewed.

After hearing my report, she shared some perspective:

> That's good! That's a successful outing. All the nice work you can do with young, undamaged horses is not like what we have here. We're looking for that 1 percent, that small but successful part of a session. You were able to unlock a physical pattern as a way of getting to the brain. That marks progress.

Getting better involves finding the scary thing, the brace, the resistance, and chipping away at its roots. The journey calls for an improved connection between brain and body. I'll undoubtedly fall off another couch and panic again in the waves. Barry will stiffen his neck and carry his head high. But baby steps and 1-percent moments still count as progress.

## Horse Owners Can Be Part of the Solution

Maybe you're like me: white and privileged enough to own horses. From our rural, mostly peaceful, mostly white communities, it might be easy to ignore the massive protests over systemic injustice. It might be easy to dismiss the protests as flash points soon to fade, bumps in the already bumpy road of 2020.

We horse owners often practice a "live and let live" philosophy, happy to stay in our lanes and keep to ourselves. What do the deaths of Black Americans in big cities have to do with us? I'm reminded of the words set in granite at the New England Holocaust Memorial in Boston, written by Martin Niemöller, a German Lutheran pastor:

They came first for the Communists,

    and I didn't speak up because I wasn't a Communist.

Then they came for the Jews,
    and I didn't speak up because I wasn't a Jew.

Then they came for the trade unionists,
    and I didn't speak up because I wasn't a trade unionist.

Then they came for the Catholics,
    and I didn't speak up because I was a Protestant.

Then they came for me,
    and by that time no one was left to speak up.

Systemic injustice is a scourge that makes its victims feel unsafe and targeted. Black Americans feel unsafe and targeted, but it could be anyone anywhere.

Systemic injustice was part of a conversation I had with Monica McWilliams 20 years ago in Boston. McWilliams co-founded the Northern Ireland Women's Coalition and won a seat in that country's original Legislative Assembly. I reported on her U.S. visit to receive a Woman of the Year award. A Catholic from South Belfast, she took part in the peace talks leading to the historic Good Friday Agreement, which largely ended the Troubles, a decades-long period of sectarian violence and political unrest affecting the United Kingdom, the Republic of Ireland, and, peripherally, the United States. Nearly 4,000 people died during the Troubles. Half were civilians.

For generations in Northern Ireland, Catholics had felt unsafe and targeted. McWilliams told me a simple story of shoe shopping. Her son was to receive his First Communion and needed white shoes to go with his outfit. Harried and in a hurry, they stopped at a shoe store in a Protestant neighborhood. Not realizing the dangerous gravity of his words, her son complained loudly about all the Communion fuss. Heads turned. Smiles turned to frowns. They were not welcome in this shop or in this neighborhood.

Systemic injustice takes all shapes in its goal to keep the powerful in power and to keep down those being dominated. The Irish know what it is. In Dublin and Belfast, they are protesting against systemic injustice after George Floyd's murder.

Sure, not all horse owners are "privileged" if we think of it in terms of socioeconomic status. I was talking about this with my friend Forrest Van Tuyl, a musician and working cowboy in Oregon. I asked him what he thought of the white privilege in the working cowboy world. "Cowboying is a choice. Being born Black is not." Privilege is not just about money advantages. It's about systemic advantages for white people that make it less likely for people of color to succeed.

If you're a woman, you know what it feels like to be targeted and unsafe. As a reporter, a runner, a laborer on construction sites, I've felt vulnerable and targeted. How about you? If you're a horse owner, you know what power and dominance look like, too. Generally, we show up for our horses with courage, support, compassion, and a sense of responsibility. But there are sickening possibilities whenever power over another being is possible: violence. Or worse, sanctioned violence. It's an ugly mix of fear, aggression, and cowardice that has hurt and killed scores of our equine partners.

Pause for a moment and think about where you cross paths with systemic injustice. It might seem like we're far removed from the treachery and pain that's unfolding today—mostly in big cities without a horse in sight—but if you look more closely, you'll see just a few degrees of separation. Ask yourself: Are you minding your own business or sticking your head in the sand? Let's counter this year's fear, ignorance, and cynicism with joy, knowledge, and compassion. Join the conversation and be part of the solution.

## Come Mayhem, How Will We Fare?

I'm a reasonable person. Like a lot of people, I'm politically centric and middle class. I have no outstanding warrants and next to no savings. I roll through stop signs and I volunteer. I'm imperfect and reasonably happy. Like lots of folks, too, I get to pondering on today's social (dis)order and unease.

Specifically, as a journalist, I get angsty about my vocation. Aside from ongoing cutbacks and layoffs by our employers, we journalists have taken physical and metaphorical beatings of late. It's troubling. When people degrade or dismiss the watchdogs and chroniclers, when they become less aware of their community functions and machinations, more unease and disorder will follow. Sometimes, when I've had too much coffee or get to talking with my friend Paul, I imagine what it'd be like if our current society got much, much more uneasy and disorderly. Mayhem in the streets! Bank closures! Food shortages!

There would be mini-mayhems, too: Will my cell phone work? How will I contact friends? Will I have access to the gym and still be able to maintain a vegan diet? Who will make my deliveries and will Uber still work? Then I remember who I am (decidedly not vegan) and where I live (where there is no Uber). Overall, I'm calm, even a little pleased with my prospects.

Let's talk about simple survival: I've put up enough wood to heat my house through winter and beyond. When the cistern (a water storage tank common to many rural properties) runs dry, I can boil snow or travel a few miles to a spring to get water. If food gets short, I can hunt and fish. (Dietarily, I'm an opportunist. I own firearms and, I suppose if things got really ugly, I could use them to defend myself.) I can drive a truck and haul a trailer. If gas runs out, I can ride my horses. If hay runs out, I can turn them loose. I can sew, knit, camp, use a chain saw, change a tire, change the oil, swing a hammer, fix things, and build fence.

That isn't boasting. Many friends have better skills, strength, and savvy. In my tiny town of 1,400, I'm familiar and friendly with a few hundred. Given my network, I could barter services with scores of talented acquaintances. When considering mayhem and mini-mayhem, though, one must think beyond survival. Let's talk about state of mind: Will we freak out at the loss of technology and Internet? Will we struggle when there's no point in looking at our phones?

Last week, after the sun was up, I got horseback and rode south. I took the dogs and traveled down the snowy canyon until it opened up. Up on a bench (a topographical feature, not a piece of furniture. This is a snippy parenthetical remark, perhaps, but nature-related words are increasingly omitted from new dictionaries, and I rue the day when "weed" no longer refers, even secondarily, to thistle, mullein, and burdock), we paused to catch our breath. It was intensely quiet. I could see a radio tower some six miles away and a plane overhead. The closest human was not close.

You know that feeling you get when your extremities are really, really cold and then they start to warm up? For a moment, it feels painful and kind of nauseating, but then fingers and toes become campfire warm. "Ow!" Then "Ohh!" Then "Ahhh!" In that moment on the bench, that's what I felt. Big country can be overwhelming like that. It can be scary, even sickening, to consider one's vulnerability and insignificance. Once acclimated through practice, though, it's invigorating to move in the wilderness. The quietness— of place and of state of mind—is lovely and warm. "Ow!" Then "Ohh!" Then "Ahhh!"

I'm comfortable in the backcountry and wish more people could unleash themselves to get energized and inspired by being alone and off-line; by using skills, strength, and MacGyverism to get through jams; and by spending time in an animate, nonhuman world. When I started writing this piece, I found myself swerving into today's usual divisive potholes: Rural living is the best; city slickers are clueless. Smartphones are destroying society. Everyone is looking in or down when they should be looking up and out. My son Aidan reminded me that today's world is more nuanced. People are complicated and their challenges are multifold.

And yet, imagine the next time we get inconvenienced by disconnect or find ourselves outside and phoneless. What a gift. "Ow!" Then "Ohh! Then "Ahhhh!" Come what may, we might all be reasonably fine.

# Fence-Sitting

The following pandemic-related essay was published in the *Colorado Sun*.

After a seven-mile ride in mud and snow, I bring the horses back to the paddock, toss them hay, and sit on the fence. Sitting on the fence is not a metaphor, it is what horse owners do as we watch, contemplate, and maybe—though it seems highly indulgent—cherish our time with *Equus caballus*. As more of us seek equine-related activities during the pandemic, fence-sitting is a thing. Horses, it seems, are reestablishing their place in society. They're also going through a rebranding: out as beasts of burden, in as beasts of being.

Parents have flocked to barns, looking to assuage their children's anxieties with riding lessons. Friends of mine who manage barns and have horses in training, now have long wait lists. Christy Landwehr, CEO of Certified Horsemanship Association, the largest certifying body in North America, with 3,500 members, told me they're struggling to keep up with demand.

Meanwhile, some horse owners, facing the choice of feeding their families or their mounts, have had to surrender horses. Rescue organizations are busy, too. Contrary to what you might think, riding and horse owning is not a country club affair, reserved solely for the rich and privileged. According to demographic research, only a third of the nation's 5 million horse owners are well off. A third are solidly middle class. A third are less well off. Many live in the country. We have stinky clothes, no vacation days, slim wallets, and weathered crow's feet on our faces, from smiling and wincing in the weather. More than any outdoor recreationalist, we are out there, in sub-zeros and triple digits, caring for and working with our equine partners.

Anecdotally, I can say that most of us have horses in the blood, passed down generously by parents and grandparents. In this corner of Colorado, families literally came to the area on horses' backs. Here, many horses need to be handy, able to work cows, move through gates, hold steady during brandings, and perform myriad tasks in shifting conditions (like storms and road traffic).

When we see the droves of newcomers to our vocation, some of us are amused. Some of us worry that newbies will treat horses as big purse dogs, accessories to their world. Horses suffer when they are put in small spaces (stalls), given meals (grain), and adorned with clothing (blankets). As director of the annual Best Horse Practices Summit, I chat with scores of well-meaning owners who run the risk of loving their new equines to death. "Let a horse be a horse" is not just a woke phrase. It's supported by research and speaks to the horse's need for freedom, friends, and forage (i.e., being able to live in a large space where they can graze most of the day and be with a herd).

Notwithstanding these educational challenges, newcomers are welcome. They've helped us better appreciate what's been there all along: a horse's presence. You can feel heat radiating from its thousand-pound body and smell its pleasant musk. You can watch its ears (which pivot independently) and eyes (the biggest in the mammalian world) as they consider you. Horse time is immersive. That's one reason it's so therapeutically effective.

Another reason is that horse work is a two-way deal in which we learn (often the hard way) about respect, trust, consistency, and boundaries. I say it's more valuable and harder to maintain than the relationships people have with dogs or cats. I say it's more profound than any gardening or yoga practice. It could be that horse-to-human work has perfectly prepared us for times of struggle, like a global pandemic and a chaotic political climate. My friend Amy Skinner shared her overall situation in North Carolina:

> I don't feel like anything has changed. I have the same amount of isolation, of not going to town, of being alone. With the horses, I'm grounded and focused and things are pleasant. All's well in the horses' world. I have had a great year. I kinda feel guilty.

Nancy Schaufele, an older friend in Utah, had this to report, after she struggled with Covid:

> I never missed a feeding. Yet some mornings I didn't know if I'd make it down the hill to the barn. As soon as I heard that soft nicker, though, I'd feel better. I think doing those chores kept me going. There is something healing about being near a warm horse body, watching the glow of a setting sun. I could have called on offers of help, but I wanted to do it as long as I could muster the strength.

To all those just now discovering horses, I say "Welcome!" While we see livestock, you see listeners. No matter the form or outcome, I root for horses to stick around. We need them now, as we have for millennia.

# CHAPTER SEVEN

# Essays on Conservation and Community

I'm grateful to the *Washington Post* and the *Colorado Sun* for publishing the following opinion pieces concerning, among other topics, the city-country disconnect. They have been expanded here for your consideration.

## Setting Politics Aside

Like so many other places, Colorado is experiencing a massive influx of new residents. Here in Montezuma County, the state's most southwestern county, home prices jumped 30 percent last year over 2019. Inventory is rock-bottom low.

Six years ago, I was one of those transplants, arriving with dogs and horses, eager for the excitement of new community and open space. Forty percent of the county is public land; some call it an outdoor paradise. Since I work from home, signing up for Internet service was one of my first priorities. After the hookup, I got online to check email. The silent beach ball of buffering was still spinning as a cup of tea went cold. I canceled the crappy service and headed to the local public library where scores of folks head for Wi-Fi.

What is essential? What makes you feel safe and comfortable? These questions are practical as well as existential when moving to a new place. As an outsider, you may not share values with your neighbors. You may not understand the local ways of life. You might miss services and amenities you took for granted.

Here, where the average income is $26,000, not far from the national poverty line, Trump and Lauren Boebert (who promised to bring her Glock to Congress and tweeted "Today is 1776" on January 6) beat their Democratic rivals by nearly 2-to-1 margins. Oil, gas, and agriculture are economic strongholds. Cattle drives can monopolize secondary roads, and even state highways, as ranchers move their stock from one pasture to another.

Here, you learn that just because there's a creek running through your property doesn't mean you can draw from it. Water is controlled by deeded rights and enforced by a "water cop," a sheriff's deputy. You learn that if cows come on your land, they're not necessarily trespassing. Colorado is a "fence-out" state. So, if you don't want livestock on your place, build fence.

You might not want a compost pile, lest you attract bears. You might get your dogs vaccinated for rattlesnake bites. Also, don't let them chase deer, elk, or cattle. They can be shot for that. You might have to run to the middle of your driveway, just south of that juniper, to talk with friends on your cell phone. Or maybe you cave and get a landline. Your neighborhood might be evacuated due to wildfire. Last year, 3,000 acres burned near me. I had less than an hour to grab my go bag, load up four horses and two dogs, and get the hell out. Within hours, giant slurry bombers were strafing the ridge, 600 yards from my home.

I credit my dogs and horses for helping me meet folks and become useful. Through years of trial and practice, of embarrassment and schooling, we now can be passably handy around livestock. Our work—in frigid cold, in bone-chilling rain, in heat, sun, and dust—sometimes has me wondering why I'd want to hunch over a laptop and write when I could be doing this all day, all month, all year. The highest compliment yet paid to me was while moving cows, when a rancher rode close and asked how much I wanted for my savvy, smooth-moving dog. I'll keep him, sir, but thank you kindly.

I visit the nearby National Forest every day for trail runs and rides. Sagebrush, grasses, piñon, and juniper cover the open, rolling hills. I can see south to New Mexico and west to Utah. I can't lie. The aloneness and need for self-reliance can be unnerving. My nearest neighbors are more than a half mile away. At night, fields of stars blossom. Coyotes' yips and howls and the wind blowing through the trees might be the only sounds interrupting the silence. Sunrise helps dispel occasional angst.

My friend Tom has lived here for nearly two decades. As program director of the local public radio station, he takes a wide-angle perspective of community: "Around here, you don't have the luxury of isolating yourself in the bubble of your own beliefs. Living here forces you to come face-to-face with a spectrum that includes gun owners, ranchers, Libertarians, and lesbians. If you're uncomfortable with that, it's not going to be fun."

Does it matter how my ranching friends voted? Not a lick. I care more about how they treat their animals and how they steward the land. More than anywhere else or at any other period of my life, I've worked to build a network of friends and acquaintances here. After a long, tiring day, they are to me like an old PayDay bar, found deep in the truck's glove compartment: salty, sweet, imperfect, and pleasing.

## Getting Out, Getting Along

Two dogs, now gone, showed me how to consider the outdoors. Belle appreciated the landscape as a whole. She stopped, not just at the summit, but to tend to sounds and smells that called to her. On each journey, she paid attention to nuances of flora and fauna. Kip, meanwhile, focused narrowly on the path and on getting somewhere. I consider people along this same continuum as they interact with the land: Some embrace it holistically, with an almost genetic sensitivity to shifts in their surroundings. Others track along, oblivious to phenomena outside their path. Among them, who are the environmentalists?

If you live in the suburbs or the city, if you're active on social platforms, if you absorb mainstream media, you might think outdoor recreationalists are the front-runners in environmentalism (which to me has fiscal, physical, and spiritual considerations).

As a kid growing up in Maine, I thought so, too. Family vacations were spent maintaining sections of the Appalachian Trail. While we fly-fished and canoed benevolently near The Forks and Kokadjo, loggers sharing the same remote roads seemed rough, and, to use today's vernacular, wholly extractive. On the waters off Harpswell, we were ceaselessly dodging lines and buoys set by lobstermen. What a hassle!

As an adult at events like the Outdoor Retailer, for which tens of thousands swarm the Colorado Convention Center, I further embraced the concept of recreationalist as environmental hero and benefactor. What outdoor company or organization doesn't espouse a *protect where we play* ethos? Surfrider Foundation and Protect Our Winters (POW), for example, are big organizations drawing recreationalists to environmentalism. The famous Banff Mountain Film Festival celebrates *mountain culture and the environment.* But do recreationalists pay it forward in any meaningful way beyond loyalty to brands like Patagonia and The North Face (which donate millions to environmental causes)?

In the rural West, it's those working the land—often conservative, Bible-carrying, gun-toting ranchers and farmers—who are doing the most impressive conservation work. After them, it's gun-and-rod-toting hunters and anglers. This goes against type and it challenges the notion that environmentalists are all left of center. It brings out the "conserve" in conservative.

Generational land wisdom and conservation efforts often sit squarely with agriculturalists. The Partnership of Rangeland Trusts (PORT), which includes farm-and-ranch-focused conservation organizations in nine western states, has conserved well over more than 3 million acres. Maggie Hanna is a senior advisor with Colorado Cattlemen's Agricultural Land Trust (CCALT), a PORT member that has conserved more than 637,000 acres. She's also a fourth-generation rancher, living within a hundred miles of a million city dwellers. These urbanites are often transient, first-generation recreationalists who may not have long-term, land-centric interests at heart, she said.

Does the mountain biker who just dropped thousands on a full-suspension rig engage in any conservation efforts? Often not. Hanna and her colleagues work to involve non-agriculturalists, and she admits that "we have to do a better job of educating and sharing our stories." Dan Malloy sees it on the water, too. "It's classic to see the average pro surfer get way more props than the ethical fisherman who is putting thousands and thousands of meals on the table," said Malloy, who surfed professionally and is an accomplished filmmaker. "Many, many people think of agriculturalists as bad guys. But these guys are not playing. They are not visiting. They are the real environmentalists."

On the fiscal side, some have proposed recreational taxes or fees to offset the imbalance of public land use. Hunters, anglers, and ranchers all pay. Hikers, bikers, and climbers may not bring home a kill, but isn't a killer day worth something? Isn't extracting an experience still extraction?

As the big multiuse season of public lands kicks into high gear, getting to know each other would help. Pete Eschallier, co-owner of Kokopelli Bike & Board, in Cortez, Colorado, loves to see National Forest trails used by all. The other day he passed or was passed by runners, horse riders, and dirt bikers. "I had the warm fuzzies. I was super happy that there was a trail system that everybody was using," said Eschallier.

Bikers may frighten and endanger horses and cows, and as part of the multiuse community, we all could do more outreach and on-trail educating. Horse and cow manure, lobster buoys and lines—they are just signs of people interacting differently. Enjoying the outdoors is not about getting your nature fix. It's not about the elevation gain or the epic selfie. It's a communion for which you should ask yourself: How did I interact? How can I give back to that which gave me such fulfillment?

## A Bad Idea for Animal Welfare

A few months ago, my friend sent an urgent text. "Call me. It's important." I called him. It was important, he said, that we go out for dinner. It was MeatOut Day, a day on which Governor Jared Polis urged Coloradans to abstain from eating meat. Unsurprisingly, in a state with nearly 40,000 farms and ranches, many groups responded with a Meat *In* Day. Here in Montezuma County, where 26,183 people and a like number of cattle are scattered over an area the size of Delaware, the Meat In response was enthusiastic. Shiloh Steak House in Cortez had a line out the door.

Now comes Initiative 16, or PAUSE ("Protect Animals from Unnecessary Suffering and Exploitation") which, if it gets on the 2022 ballot and is approved by voters, will make it excruciatingly hard for ranchers and veterinarians to take care of livestock and make a living without facing potential charges.

Introduced by two Denver-area animal rights activists, Initiative 16 could make it an illegal "sexual act" to artificially inseminate a cow or to check that a cow is pregnant. It would require ranchers and farmers to keep their livestock for years longer than is current practice. Cows, five years. Chickens, two. Critics, including scores of county commissioners and the state's veterinary association, say it's radical and egregious. A coalition has asked the state Supreme Court to review it.

I'm dismayed that yet another issue is cutting so divisively along urban-rural lines. I'm disheartened by this initiative that on its face seems all about animal welfare, but which would, in fact, precipitate worse care and outcomes. As a ballot initiative, like the wolf reintroduction measure passed last year by a fraction of a percent, PAUSE can appeal directly to the hearts of city dwellers and suburbanites whose numbers are many and whose interaction with livestock is distant and digital. Agriculturalists, here and also in Oregon, where a similar initiative may make next year's ballot, are worried and feeling under attack.

In my observation, voters who support animal rights also may think creatures need clothes and supplements and kisses; horses belong in stalls; dogs go in purses and crates. It may suit a lifestyle, but it's wrong. Anthropomorphism, I'd argue, has introduced suffering of incalculable scale. My heart goes out to horses sweating under blankets and choking down grain, and to dogs, especially of working breeds, living out isolated, sedentary years as couch companions.

"People who haven't been raised around livestock or working animals have a natural instinct to revert to the human perspective," said Dr. Sheryl King, professor emerita at Southern Illinois University, where she directed the Equine Science program. "In a way, I feel sorry for them. These are people who love animals but don't understand them." Is a longer life a better life? Is a coddled life a better life? Shall those most removed from raising animals be the arbiters of lives well lived?

That city folks could wrest control over the very real, thoughtful decisions around animals' lives and deaths doesn't seem fair. It's like empowering someone like me, who rolls through a single stop sign on the 20-mile trip to town, to make decisions around city traffic and commuting: *Let's put a gate here and a cattle guard there. Let's make exit ramps and parking garages waaaay bigger so they can accommodate those of us hauling stock trailers. Why are these roads paved anyway? Gravel would be fine.*

This is not a stay-out-of-our-business gripe. I invite anyone to explore the world in which decisions around life, death, and preventing suffering are made every day, several times a day. Working with dogs, horses, and other livestock has given me a decent understanding of stress, for instance, and how my behavior can impact animals in the moment and down the road. Stress is bad. For a rancher, a stressed cow gains less weight and is therefore less valuable. It's in ranchers' best interest to minimize stress in everything they do. Slipping cows a CBD treat is not a solution. How stressed are your animals? Would you know what to look for?

Scientists like Dr. Frans de Waal and Dr. Temple Grandin have chastised their peers for their anthropocentric approaches, in which studies and practices are well-designed for researchers but not for the elephants or cows or chimps under consideration. By spending lots of time and by observing intimately, we can better serve these creatures, they've said. Surely, the livestock industry benefits from scrutiny, but not from those who don't know that cows stand up butt-first, horses headfirst.

*Afternote: The Colorado Supreme Court unanimously ruled that the Title Board was incorrect in giving Initiative 16 the green light to proceed.*

## An Evening Ride

*Rejection, in a relationship or a work thing or whatever, is a pretty sucky deal. Negative emotions pop to the fore pretty quick: frustration, resentment, sadness.*

*So you grab your horse to head out into the evening. Except your horse scoots through the gate and then decides he doesn't like your hat. Like, really doesn't like your hat. 'Course it's not the dang hat. It's the bad juju you brought to the paddock and to the moment. Rather than jerk the line another time, you apologize, take a breath, and thank him for the check.*

*Since you started off wrong-footed, you get to spend most of the ride reassuring him that you are not a total jerk and that you really do work well together, up hills, through brush, across ledge. Gradually, he might come around to agree, but letting him pause and graze still seems as though he is doing you a favor.*

*Thanks, Barry, I needed that.*

# Afterword

We are not the same riders or people we were a decade ago. Surely, we hope we're better, but sometimes we can be oblivious to our shortcomings: *Whaddya mean I'm riding crooked? Whaddya mean I raised my voice?*

This book has asked you to embrace doubt. I'm not talking about the kind of doubt that's all hesitation and insecurity. I'm talking about inspirational doubt. Think of doubt as wonder, curiosity, experimentation, and trial and error. Think of doubt as that unnerving, maybe daunting, jumping-off point that brings you to a new level of understanding and proficiency.

One of my favorite poets, Wislawa Szymborska, said she highly valued the little phrase "I don't know." "It's small," she said, "but it flies on mighty wings. It expands our lives to include the spaces within us as well as the outer expanses." The journey to knowing is like a Maine backroad. Sometimes delightful, sometimes twisty and confounding, but always worth the trip.

# Acknowledgments

I'm grateful to the many beings who have allowed me time and experience to consider the topics here. I'm blessed to have friends and family in my world, folks who value straight talk, who are passionate about their work, and who recognize that lifting each other up is part of life's journey. Thanks, y'all, for being you and for sharing your time.

On the writing side, thanks go to Mark Stevens, Aidan Gaughran, Cormick Gaughran, Kevin Simpson at the *Colorado Sun*, Mark Lasswell at the *Washington Post*, Sam W. Butcher, Sam S. Butcher, Whit Hibbard of the *Stockmanship Journal*, and particularly to my editor Karen Haverkamp. On the riding side, I'm grateful to Amy Skinner, Katrin Silva, Geno Samora, and Justin Reichert. Thanks to friends Chris Gaggia, Nicole Grady, Zach Rhoades, Forrest Van Tuyl, and talented artist and graphic designer Jody Chapel, who helped with book design. Additional thanks go to interviewees including Dr. Virgil DiBiase, Dr. Steve Peters, West Taylor, Warwick Schiller, Kyla Strange, Mark Rashid, Joe Morris, Steve Budiansky, and to Beau Gaughran, who also contributed photos.

And, of course, four-legged friends deserve thanks and rubs for all that they've done and continue to do, making my wallet thinner and my world richer every day.

# Citations and Resources

Almossawi, Ali. *An Illustrated Book of Bad Arguments*. [New York: JasperCollins Publishers], 2013. https://bookofbadarguments.com/.

Baldwin, Ann. https://physiology.arizona.edu/person/ann-baldwin-phd.

Budiansky, Steve. http://www.budiansky.com/home.html.

Butcher, Maddy. "'Getting Out, Getting Along' Should Be Our Common Environmental Mantra." https://coloradosun.com/2021/05/16/opinion-getting-out-getting-along-maddy-butcherour-common-environmental-mantra/.

———. "For Colorado Fence-Sitters Like Me, the Coronavirus Reinforced a Love for Our Equine Companions." https://coloradosun.com/2021/03/15/write-on-colorado-maddy-butcher-3-3./.

———. "Somehow, by the Grace of God, I Weathered the Most Recent Coronavirus Storm." https://coloradosun.com/2020/12/29/write-on-colorado-maddy-butcher-3-2/.

———. "What My Horse Taught Me about Working through the Difficulties of Coronavirus." https://coloradosun.com/2020/08/21/write-on-colorado-maddy-butcher-3/.

———. "Of Whoopie Pies and Wilderness, and How Isolation Robbed Me of My Ability to Focus." https://coloradosun.com/2020/04/17/write-on-colorado-maddy-butcher-2/.

———. "Even with Orange Juice, the Coronavirus Has Turned My Thought Process into a Baggage Carousel." https://coloradosun.com/2020/04/06/write-on-colorado-maddy-butcher/.

———. "Out Here, Red or Blue Politics Doesn't Matter As Much As How You Treat Your Animals." https://www.washingtonpost.com/opinions/2021/03/01/out-here-red-or-blue-politics-doesnt-matter-much-how-you-treat-your-animals/.

———. "The Gulf between Urban and Rural Coloradans Is Widening in a Battle over Livestock." https://www.washingtonpost.com/opinions/2021/06/15/battle-over-livestock-is-latest-beef-between-urban-rural-coloradans/.

Flatt, Andrew. https://hrvtraining.com/.

Iigaya, Kiyohito, Madalena S. Fonseca, Masayoshi Murakami, Zachary F. Mainen, and Peter Dayan. "An Effect of Serotonergic Stimulation on Learning Rates for Rewards Apparent After Long Intertrial Intervals." *Nature Communications* 9, no. 2477 (2018). https://www.nature.com/articles/s41467-018-04840-2.pdf.

Hecht, Erin. https://heb.fas.harvard.edu/people/erin-hecht.

Hunt, Lynne, and Denise Chalmers, eds. *University Teaching in Focus: A Learning-Centred Approach.* London: Routledge, 2012. https://doi.org/10.4324/9780203079690.

Mason, Peggy. https://neurobiology.uchicago.edu/faculty/peggy-mason-phd.

Morris, Joe. https://morrisgrassfed.com/.

Norton, Quinn. "A World We Built to Burn." *Emptywheel,* October 18, 2019. https://www.emptywheel.net/2019/10/18/a-world-we-built-to-burn/.

Porges, Stephen. https://www.stephenporges.com/.

Rancher-to-Rancher. https://soilcarboncoalition.org/R2R/.

Schonbrun, Zach. *The Performance Cortex: How Neuroscience Is Redefining Athletic Genius.* New York: Dutton, 2018.

Schulz, Kathryn. *Being Wrong: Adventures in the Margin of Error.* New York: Ecco, 2010.

Silva, Katrin. https://www.katrinsilvadressage.com/.

Skinner, Amy. https://amyskinnerhorsemanship.com/.

Taylor, West. https://westtaylor.net/.

Tracey, Irene. https://www.ndcn.ox.ac.uk/team/irene-tracey.

Twilley, Nicola. "The Neuroscience of Pain." *The New Yorker,* June 25, 2018.

https://www.newyorker.com/magazine/2018/07/02/the-neuroscience-of-pain.

Van der Kolk, Bessel A. *The Body Keeps the Score: Brain, Mind, and Body in the Healing of Trauma*. New York: Viking Penguin, 2014.

Vedantam, Shankar. "In the Heat of the Moment: How Intense Emotions Transform Us." *Hidden Brain*, December 2, 2019. https://www.npr.org/transcripts/783495595.

———. "Facts Aren't Enough: The Psychology of False Beliefs." *Hidden Brain*, July 22, 2019.

https://www.npr.org/transcripts/743195213.

Welland, Elaine. http://www.cowboyallday.com/.

# About the Author

Maddy Butcher is the founder and publisher of Cayuse Communications, a family of websites for horse and outdoor enthusiasts. She is the executive director of the Best Horse Practices Summit, an annual conference with academic and arena presentations that enlighten and inform the horse-human connection. An award-winning blogger, Butcher has contributed to the *Washington Post*, *High Country News*, the *Colorado Sun*, the *Boston Globe*, and the *Wall Street Journal*. She authored *A Rider's Reader: Exploring Horse Sense, Science & Sentiment* and *Horse Head: Brain Science & Other Insights*. The Maine native currently lives in Colorado.

Made in the USA
Columbia, SC
07 October 2021